Birds of Coast and Sea
Britain and Northern Europe

Birds of Coast and Sea
Britain and Northern Europe

BRUCE CAMPBELL

Illustrations by RAYMOND WATSON

Oxford

Oxford University Press

Toronto

1977

Oxford University Press,
Walton Street, Oxford OX2 6DP

Oxford London Glasgow New York
Toronto Melbourne Wellington Cape Town
Ibadan Nairobi Dar es Salaam Lusaka
Addis Ababa Kuala Lumpur Singapore
Jakarta Hong Kong Tokyo Delhi Bombay
Calcutta Madras Karachi

First published 1977

This book was designed and produced by
George Rainbird Ltd,
36 Park Street, London W1Y 4DE

'House Editor: Curigwen Lewis
Designer: Patrick Yapp

ISBN 0 19 217661 7

The text was set, printed and bound by
W. S. Cowell Ltd, Ipswich, Suffolk
The colour plates were originated by
Gilchrist Bros. Ltd, Leeds and printed by
W. S. Cowell Ltd

PRINTED IN ENGLAND

Contents

Foreword

I suppose it is only natural that the people of Northern Europe, whose countries have long and varied coast lines, should hold seabirds in especial regard. After all most of us like to spend our holidays by the sea and to some degree take an interest in the unfamiliar birdlife found there. Even if this is sometimes taken for granted and all the varied birds designated simply as seagulls, there is no doubt that they do at least form a vital ingredient of the change of scene.

Those who are more discerning and stop to take a closer look may well find themselves hooked on an abiding interest with an important new dimension of life opening before them.

In my case it was not until I reached the age of 35 that I began to find feathered birds of any more than passing interest. It may not have been entirely coincidental that this dawning followed closely upon my marriage. Now marriage is a state which besides concentrating a man's mind also behoves him to confine himself to strictly aerial flights of fancy. In addition it so happened that round about this time, soon after the war, my wife and I inherited a small cottage on the coast of Suffolk. It was situated at one of England's most easterly points on a deserted stretch of coast with reed-beds and marsh stretching away inland. The whole area seemed to belong to the birds.

The keen invigorating East Anglian air is highly conducive to brisk movement and soon I found myself taking solitary walks along the foreshore with our two dogs. I must say it would have taken a very dull dog indeed to have ignored the teeming bird-life to be seen there.

I was first entranced by the Little Terns – those swallows of the sea. It was impossible to disregard their elegant, buoyant flight – and the intensity with which they scanned the surface – bills downturned. Every now and again one would hover daintily on streamlined wings before plummeting down with a splash. It would then instantly re-appear to resume its restless vigil over the waves.

One bright spring morning I came upon an area of foreshore where a dozen or so of these delightful little creatures were flying around in high excitement uttering their strident cries. In the bright yellow bills of some I saw the silvery glint of a tiny fish.

This puzzled me for a time as the fish was not swallowed but borne importantly. Soon I realized I was seeing part of the courting display in which the males proudly present a fish to their chosen mates. It was evident that I had stumbled upon a breeding colony.

All doubts were removed when I very nearly trod on three eggs deposited in a scrape among the sand and shingle. They blended so perfectly with their surroundings that they were almost impossible to see. By now the birds were swooping low over my head trying to scare me away. I took the hint and left them in peace. How sad to think that today, some 25 years later, the Little Tern has become one of Britain's rarer breeding seabirds.

It was a little odd that it should have been a tern that first caught my attention. Strangely enough it was one of the MacDougall clan who first identified a new species of tern – the Roseate – in 1812. Of course those were days when seabirds were indiscriminately hunted and a naturalist would scarcely hesitate to shoot any bird he thought of interest.

On this occasion a Dr MacDougall of Glasgow with a party of 'sportsmen' was visiting an island in Millport Bay in the Firth of Clyde. Soon they singled out some unusual-looking terns and promptly shot them out of the sky, although we are told 'several escaped wounded'.

On inspection in the hand, the tiny victims were seen to have a rosy suffusion of the breast. The intrepid doctor duly sent one to Colonel George Montagu who promptly named the new species of tern – *Sterna dougallii*. Thus was immortality secured and I can now preen myself in the distantly reflected glory from my namesake.

Today all seabirds are under threat and none more so than terns. Their preference for nesting on the sand and shingle of the foreshore makes them especially vulnerable to interference from the pressure of holiday-makers and caravanners. The once rarely frequented beaches of Suffolk I know so well are no exception. It is fortunate that one of the principal reserves of the Royal Society for the Protection of Birds is situated at Minsmere on the north Suffolk coast, where a hundred different kinds of bird can breed undisturbed.

Here there have been many triumphs of conservation and management. In a shallow man-made lagoon a short distance back from the shore-line numerous islands have been constructed with different surfaces to attract a variety of breeding birds. In all 1500 pairs have been added to the reserve and among them hundreds of terns, refugees from their disturbed breeding grounds on the foreshore.

Here, too, as many as 30 different species of wader can be seen at the peak time in late July and early August on passage from their breeding grounds further north in Europe. They are attracted by the rich supply of food available in the brackish water and mud where the salinity is carefully controlled by a system of fresh-water sluices. My old friend Herbert Axell, who created this splendid area known as 'the scrape' when he was the warden in charge at Minsmere, described this rich food as a living soup for birds. This has also certainly led to the establishment of a breeding colony of Avocets – the elegant black and white wader which is the emblem of the R.S.P.B.

Another heartening conservation victory has taken place on the north-west coast of England, at Morecambe Bay. This might at a glance seem the unlikeliest of places. Morecambe itself is, of course, a popular holiday resort, but just at the end of the promenade in spring and early summer you can see one of the finest ornithological sights in Europe. The 120 square miles of intertidal sandflats form the most important estuary for birds in Britain and one of the most important in Europe. It is a vast larder of natural food – bivalves, sandhoppers, marine snails and worms attracting waders in tens of thousands. In mid-winter Knot and Dunlin predominate but there are also large numbers of Curlew, Redshank, Turnstone and Bar-tailed Godwit. In April and May the wintering birds are joined by a host of passage migrants that winter further south and there may be as many as 100,000 at a time. How good it is to know that at a time when the shorelines of Europe are shrinking under a tide of industrial development, the R.S.P.B. has been able to acquire 6000 acres of estuary which now form one of its latest and largest reserves.

Since my interest in seabirds was first aroused, I have delighted in the sight of them all over the world, never more so than on a recent crossing of the Pacific when our ship was escorted over thousands of miles by a number of Black-browed Albatrosses. I never tired of watching these great birds manoeuvring gracefully on the air currents in our wake; sometimes they would peel off and, with dark narrow wings full spread, scythe low over the furrowed sea.

This book I know will be the perfect introduction for newcomers to the subject and be equally welcome to those already captivated by the fascination and mystery surrounding the lives of our birds of the sea and open shore – many of which spend nearly all their lives quartering the vast expanses of the oceans of the world.

We know a fair amount about their breeding behaviour, but scarcely anything from the moment each year when they glide away from the crowded cliff tops or island colonies to spend the following months at sea.

Dr Bruce Campbell is the ideal person to provide the text for this book, being not only one of Britain's foremost ornithologists but also exceptionally endowed with the gift of communication. He is himself an experienced broadcaster and for three years headed the B.B.C. Natural History Unit at Bristol. When his skills are combined with the meticulous observation and superb craftsmanship of a bird artist of the calibre of Raymond Watson – then you have a book of rare quality.

It is also appearing at an ideal time because surely one of the more hopeful features all over Europe during the past few years has been the greatly increased interest in all aspects of wildlife and birdlife in particular. I suppose it is when the news is at its bleakest and most negative that we turn with relief to the enduring positive things of life. How good it is to know that with the numerous man-made threats hanging over the continued existence of seabirds there is now throughout Europe an enlightened public opinion, which increasingly demands that they be given more protection. What a long way we have come since the last century when the persecution of birds was such that it is only to be wondered that more species were not harried to extinction, as was the Great Auk. So successfully had these birds adapted to the sea that finally they lost the power of flight. This left them at the mercy of fishermen who proceeded to slaughter them ruthlessly for food and bait. Although at one time they bred on low-lying rocky islands from Newfoundland to Iceland – their last stronghold, on the Faeroe Islands, St Kilda, and probably elsewhere off the coasts of Britain and Ireland, by 1844 the Great Auk was no more.

On many coastal settlements seabirds and their eggs had long been regarded as an essential supply of food. I was reminded of this recently on a visit to the flower-strewn, red sandstone clifftop of St Bees Head which juts out into the Irish Sea opposite the Isle of Man. Here in Cumbria just two miles south from the busy industrial port of Whitehaven is one of the most important sites for seabirds in England, and the only place where all four members of the auk family breed. Guillemots, Razorbills, Puffins and Black Guillemots return to these cliffs each year to lay their eggs and rear their chicks. They now have security of tenure because a three-mile stretch of the cliff forms another of the reserves recently acquired by the R.S.P.B.

The reminder that it was not always so came from the landlord of a nearby village inn. He had lived there man and boy for over 60 years and well remembered the local men bringing in to the pub great baskets piled high with Guillemot eggs.

Away on the other side of England too, at Bempton on the Yorkshire coast just west of Flamborough Head, the R.S.P.B. has bought a three-mile stretch of the white chalk cliffs, which rise 350 feet sheer from the sea, and established a reserve which is manned by a warden throughout the breeding season. This is the home of 60,000 seabirds, with one of the largest Kittiwake colonies, and the only place where Gannets breed on the mainland of Britain. Normally they prefer island sites. Here they can now breed undisturbed, but not so long ago local men and boys made perilous descents by rope each year to gather the 'harvest' of eggs. This practice was known locally as 'climming'. By the turn of the century 130,000 Guillemot eggs were being taken annually. Some were for local consumption but the bulk of them ended up in Leeds where, I'm told, the albumen was used to help put the shine in patent leather.

It must not be thought however that Britain's historical attitude to seabirds was solely one of persecution. No less a person than James Fisher, who was Chairman of the Seabird Group set up in 1965 to take a census of breeding seabirds, maintained that a poem, 'The Seafarer', written some 1300 years ago referred to the Bass Rock at the mouth of the Firth of Forth. In the poem, a young Anglo-Saxon, no doubt a little world-weary and wanting to get away from it all, describes vividly his feelings on visiting the area in spring:

> There heard I naught but seething sea,
> Ice-cold wave, awhile a song of swan.
> There came to charm me gannets' pother
> And whimbrels' trills for the laughter of men,
> Kittiwake singing instead of mead.
> Storms there the stacks thrashed, there answered them
>   the tern
> With icy feathers; full oft the erne wailed round
> Spray-feathered . . .

The erne refers to the White-tailed or Sea Eagle which was once quite common round British coasts.

It was fitting that when James Fisher died tragically in a car accident in 1970 his many naturalist friends came together and launched a joint appeal for the purchase of an island nature reserve in his memory. Two years later the sea-lashed island of Copinsay off the Mainland of Orkney was bought and is now administered by the R.S.P.B. The Vikings knew it as Kolbeinsay (Kolbein's Island); the Celts knew it before them. Today the sheer cliffs where hosts of seabirds glide and wheel perpetuate the memory of James Maxwell McConnell Fisher.

It was apt too that when he was Chairman of the Seabird Group he should have suggested that the national census of breeding birds be called 'Operation Seafarer' – the name of the Anglo-Saxon poem he had translated.

But just why was 'Operation Seafarer' necessary at all? I well remember seeing a cartoon one day in *The Times* of two desperate shipwrecked mariners on a raft. One was dipping his hand into the water as he said to his companion in distress: 'We must be nearing civilization – this water is polluted'.

A few years later Thor Heyerdahl, after his crossing of the Atlantic on a papyrus raft, told a shocked world on his return that he saw no part of that great ocean entirely free of contamination by oil. More recently still, on 24 April 1975, at the 138-nation Geneva Conference on the law of the sea Dr Jacques Cousteau, the eminent French ocean explorer, demanded 'drastic action' to save the sea – and the human race – from the danger of death in a few decades. As he said: 'Ecologists know very well that the human species cannot survive if the oceans die. We are talking about the survival of our children', and he concluded, 'the oceans could be dead in less than 50 years.'

Over the past ten years two events in particular have alerted public opinion in this country to the danger. First there was that disaster which, as a B.B.C. television news-reader, it sickened me to have to broadcast on 18 March 1967. To save 29 minutes the captain of an oil tanker had sailed inside rather than outside the Isles of Scilly and had slammed his ship onto the Seven Stones Reef off Land's End. It could not have happened at a worse time. Within three days slicks of crude oil the colour of melted chocolate were spreading over a hundred square miles of ocean and ensnaring huge numbers of auks which are always moving through these waters at that time of year. A week later thousands of seabirds, some just corpses, others still struggling helplessly in their strait-jackets of Kuwait crude oil were being swept in along a hundred miles of Cornwall's finest beaches. In spite of a great campaign, almost on a war footing, to clear up the mess, something like 20,000 auks died slow and horrible deaths.

The second major disaster came two years later. If less dramatic as a news story, it was in fact even more significant as a pointer to the way in which the oceans of the world are being insidiously poisoned. During the autumn months of 1969 the corpses of over 15,000 guillemots and other seabirds were found on the beaches on both sides of the Irish Sea. The puzzling thing was that very few of them were oiled. After an exhaustive inquiry no definite conclusion was reached as to the cause of their deaths although residues of many substances were found in some of the bodies analysed, ranging from organochlorine pesticides to a variety of metals. Also present were high levels of polychorinated biphenyls, or PCBs, used in the manufacture of some transformers, plastics and paints.

It is clear that we can no longer think of the sea as a safe dumping ground vast enough to absorb even the most toxic industrial wastes. In this respect seabirds can provide an invaluable first warning when something is wrong with the marine environment. 'Operation Seafarer' was necessary in order that the nesting sites of seabirds in Britain and Ireland might be located and their numbers estimated. Without this knowledge it was impossible to assess

11

with any accuracy how the various species were faring.

In addition the information was needed as a base-line against which future changes could be measured. That may sound simple enough but the difficulties in counting colonies of breeding birds on inaccessible cliff sites or on remote sea-girt stacks off the coast of Scotland and Ireland were formidable indeed. After surveys and reconnaissance in 1967 and 1968 the main census was carried out the following year by volunteer observers, the whole operation being masterminded by David Saunders, formerly Warden on Skomer off the coast of south Wales. The report (see Introduction) gives fairly precise figures for 17 of the 24 species of British seabird, and estimates the total numbers breeding on the coast at some three million pairs – a considerably lower figure than expected.

As an adjunct to 'Operation Seafarer', the R.S.P.B. has organized Beached Bird Surveys in which hundreds of volunteers comb a thousand miles of coastline round the British Isles each year. The main value of the surveys is that they give an indication of seabird mortality in normal conditions and make it possible to measure the gravity and extent of the major disasters when they come. Razorbills, guillemots, divers, and ducks such as Common Scoter and Eider, have been found to be the most frequent victims of oil. The surveys now extend to the European coastline where similar counts have been made on the beaches of Denmark, Holland, Germany, Belgium and France.

As a result of all this effort what has been learnt about the way seabird populations are faring? The surprising thing is that five species (Gannet, Fulmar, Kittiwake, Herring Gull, and Great Skua) have considerably increased in numbers; four (Shag, Cormorant, Great Black-backed Gull and Black-headed Gull) have increased in some areas and decreased elsewhere; and for three species (Sandwich Tern, Common Gull and Lesser Black-backed Gull) it is thought that there has probably been an overall increase. On the other hand the Little Tern has decreased greatly and it is suspected that overall declines have taken place in the numbers of Guillemots, Razorbills and Puffins. For Common, Arctic and Roseate Terns there is no definite conclusion though they too are thought to have declined in recent years.

Of the remaining species the trends for the Arctic Skua remain uncertain and almost nothing is known about the population of Manx Shearwaters, Storm Petrels and Leach's Petrels owing to the fact that they are largely nocturnal and nest in burrows on remote, inaccessible sites.

The fact that some seabirds are increasing in numbers may partly be due to a more intensive fishing industry. Fleets of trawlers equipped with radar and sonic devices now range ever more widely over the oceans. Certainly Fulmars and gulls find an abundant food supply in the offal discarded in harbours and at sea. On the other hand a trawler's nets will catch diving birds as well as fish and the nylon from which the nets are now made is almost impossible to see. This may well be a contributory reason for the decline in auks. There have even been occasional reports from the west Greenland salmon fisheries of more birds being caught than fish.

There remains the one great imponderable which hangs over the fate of so many of our birds of the sea and open shore – the crucial off-shore oil industry. Here Britain, Norway and other countries of Northern Europe have a big international responsibility. Hosts of seabirds from vast areas of ocean breed off their coasts and in addition the relatively mild climate of Britain and Ireland attracts wintering flocks of wild fowl and waders from their distant northern breeding grounds. All these birds may soon be at risk.

Apart from the dangers to birdlife, it is surely unthinkable that we should allow the incomparable beaches, bays and inlets of the Highlands and Islands to be desecrated by oil pollution and industrial development.

Three wildlife conservation bodies have fortunately been closely involved in events so far in Scotland. The Nature Conservancy Council, although the statutory body, has only slender resources and so its work is supplemented by the Scottish Wildlife Trust and the R.S.P.B. Their efforts have been directed to attempts to plan development so that, when the oil begins to flow, harm to the natural environment will be prevented or kept to a minimum. In most cases the best that can be hoped for is a compromise.

Most of the oil will be brought ashore by pipeline but some will come by tanker. We know that pipelines are liable to failure from a variety of causes and occasional leaks of oil seem inevitable. As for tankers, where loading and unloading operations are always liable to human error or equipment failure, spillages sooner or later are almost certain. This is to say nothing of the risk of a major disaster such as a well blow-out or rig fire.

It is of some comfort to know that the United Kingdom Offshore Operators Association has assured conservation bodies that all spills caused by the operations of its members will be treated immediately. Unfortunately the dispersal of oil at sea is a very much more difficult and costly procedure than some theories suggest. The cost of cleaning up after the *Torrey Canyon* disaster was £1,400,000 and of the 8000 oiled birds rescued only a mere hundred or so recovered sufficiently to be returned to the sea. Of these 60 were ringed before release and within a few weeks 16 of them were found dead. The conclusion then was that only the most lightly oiled birds ever have any chance of survival and that in future the most humane treatment for the others was to collect them and destroy them under expert supervision.

Happily as a result of investigations made at the Research Unit in Newcastle upon Tyne, together with more recent experience, new treatment methods have now been developed which allow many birds to be returned to sea within a few weeks. Although these methods have given encouraging results, there is no foolproof method of treating oiled birds. Circumstances differ from one spill to the next and different species present different problems. It is essentially a skilled task and requires certain basic facilities which are only likely to be available at a few centres. Amongst other things plentiful supplies of piped hot and cold water are essential.

As this splendid book will show Northern Europe's seabirds and birds of the open shore are a priceless heritage. Although great strides have been made towards their conservation in this century and particularly over the past ten years or so, the next few years may be even more crucial.

We must learn to temper our need for technological development so that we do not lose that wild beauty without which life would lose so much of its savour.

John Ruskin, one of the wisest of the nineteenth-century thinkers once wrote:

God has lent us the earth for our life, it is a great entail, it belongs as much to those who are to come after us as to us and we have no right by anything we do or neglect to involve them in any unnecessary penalties or deprive them of the benefit which was in our power to bequeath.

How much truer are his words for us today.

ROBERT DOUGALL

Introduction

Any book that does not aim to cover the whole bird life of a region faces problems of selection. The primary criterion for inclusion in this book has been regular occurrence at some season along the coast of Europe and its islands, from Brittany to the frontier with Asia. But the number of species that turn up on such a long and convoluted coastline runs into hundreds, so a restriction was made in favour of birds that live all or much of their lives on the shore or at sea.

Even then there had to be exclusions, the most painful being that of the surface-feeding or dabbling ducks, some of which winter, often in very large numbers, on estuaries and sheltered shores. So no Wigeon, even though shortly before writing these words I had been watching several thousands of them grazing with White-fronted and Canada Geese (both included) just inland from the Severn estuary in Gloucestershire.

On the other hand, some readers may feel we have included waders that are only marginally coastal. But if the Common Sandpiper, clearly a bird of sheltered coasts in Northern Europe, claims a place, it seems justifiable on comparative grounds to add Green and Wood Sandpipers.

Outside what are fairly obviously 'water birds', only two species have been included, the Shore Lark because its ecology is convergent with that of several waders and the Rock Pipit because of its unique adaptation to a littoral life. Strong cases could also be made for several birds of prey and 'corvids' and for the Rock Dove, *Columbia livia*, but the line had to be drawn somewhere and I think Raymond Watson's 64 paintings and many drawings, to which I have been honoured to try to fit a text, are sufficient of a feast within one pair of covers.

Birds may have two or three scientific names in Latin form: the generic distinguished by an initial capital letter, followed by the specific and sometimes by a sub-specific or racial name, without capital initials. I have tried to be sparing with these last but some were inevitable and are usually prefaced by 'the race' or 'the sub-species'. For generic and specific names I have followed the British Trust for Ornithology's *A Species List of British and Irish Birds*, edited by Robert Hudson. Each species is introduced in the text by its specific name, followed by the most generally accepted English name and by the family, after which the total length (bill to tail) in centimetres is given. I have tried to avoid technical terms, except for plumage areas, to which keys appear on p. 17. There is a short glossary on p. 18. All the species described have only a single brood annually unless otherwise stated.

As regards geographical terms, I have frequently used the expression 'the arctic archipelagos' for the island groups north of the arctic circle (in accordance with Norse usage Svalbard covers the whole group of which Spitsbergen is the largest island); by 'the Atlantic Islands' are meant the groups off Northwest Africa (e.g. Madeira, Canaries, Azores) which are sometimes mentioned in accounts of passage or wintering.

Our first acknowledgement must be to Robert Dougall for writing a foreword which so well communicates his affection for sea birds, deals so adequately with the conservation issue and sets the tone for the whole book. Raymond Watson would like to thank the Castle Museum, Norwich and particularly Jeremy Heath, Curator of Natural History at the Colchester and Essex Museum, for the unstinted help given with specimen skins.

John Parslow, now Deputy Director (Conservation) of the Royal Society for the Protection of Birds, read through the whole text and made many valuable suggestions which I was happy to incorporate; Euan Dunn kindly commented on the terns and Ævar Petersen on the Black Guillemot, on which he is making a special study. Of written sources I found A. J. Prater's reports on the Birds of Estuaries Enquiry (especially that for 1972–3) most helpful. So were three recent books, *The Seabirds of Britain and Ireland* (Collins, 1974), by Stanley Cramp, W. R. P. Bourne and David Saunders; this embodies the report on Operation Seafarer held in 1969–70; *Ducks of Britain and Europe* (Poyser, 1975) by M. A. Ogilvie; and *A Field Guide to the Nests, Eggs and Nestlings of British and European Birds* (Collins, 1975) by Colin Harrison. I also found myself returning again and again to *The Handbook of British Birds* (Witherby, 1938–41) and to B. W. Tucker's unrivalled field descriptions, from which I could not resist several quotations. I have drawn heavily as well on K. H. Voous's *Atlas of European Birds* (Nelson, 1960). In addition I consulted many books and papers in the Alexander Library of the Edward Grey Institute, Oxford University Department of Zoology, with much help from Dorothy Vincent, until recently its custodian. But with so much active study, particularly of arctic-breeding waders, in progress, and awaiting publication, it is impossible for the text to be as up-to-date with developments as I should have wished.

Finally, I have been happy to work with Raymond Watson, an artist and ornithologist of great perception, and with Curigwen Lewis who has patiently shouldered the endless chores of a house editor. Anne Bell performed the feat of extracting a final typing from my vermicular drafts.

BRUCE CAMPBELL

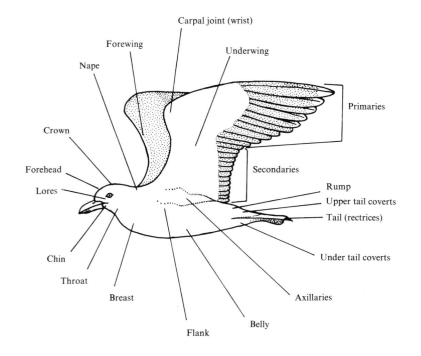

Carpal joint (wrist)

Forewing

Underwing

Nape

Primaries

Crown

Forehead

Secondaries

Lores

Rump

Upper tail coverts

Tail (rectrices)

Chin

Under tail coverts

Throat

Breast

Axillaries

Belly

Flank

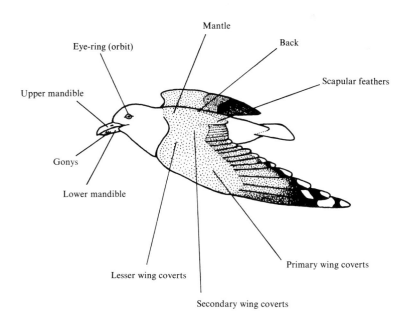

Mantle

Eye-ring (orbit)

Back

Scapular feathers

Upper mandible

Gonys

Lower mandible

Primary wing coverts

Lesser wing coverts

Secondary wing coverts

17

Glossary

(with acknowledgments to *A New Dictionary of Birds*, edited by A. Landsborough Thomson)

Brood Patch Bare area on the underside of a bird, richly supplied with blood vessels and through which heat is transferred from the parent to the eggs or small young.

Dread Sudden mass movement away from the breeding colony, particularly characteristic of terns; see under Arctic Tern (plate 57).

Eclipse Short plumage phase, especially characteristic of male ducks, assumed after mating in summer, generally resembling that of the female and coinciding with moulting of the flight feathers.

Flirting Rapid movements of wings or tail, notably when a bird is agitated.

Pad Nest Simple nest of grass stems and other local vegetation as built by many waders.

Pipped Term used for first chipping of the shell by the chick before it hatches.

Pitching Landing, especially of birds on water.

Rodent Run Form of distraction display in which parent attempts to lure intruder away from nest or young by giving impression of small mammal; see under Purple Sandpiper (plate 38).

Speculum Area of distinctive colour, usually confined to the secondary feathers of the wing; especially the metallic patch characteristic of certain ducks.

Tarsus or Shank More correctly the tarsometatarsus, the leg bone formed by fusion of tarsal and metatarsal elements.

Trip 'Noun of assembly' used for Dotterel; cf. 'spring' of Teal, 'skein' of geese on the wing.

Triumph Ceremony Display, first described by Oskar Heinroth at the Fifth International Ornithological Congress, between members of a pair of geese or other waterfowl after driving off an intruder; both birds shake their wings and call loudly.

Whiffling Term used by wildfowlers for the 'spiral nose-dive with wings half-folded and side-slipping in a remarkable manner' (B. W. Tucker), performed especially by flocks of grey geese.

Index

Numbers after each entry are plate numbers. **Bold** numbers indicate that the species is illustrated in colour, *italic* numbers that it is shown in black and white. Species illustrated in colour may also be shown in black and white. Numbers in roman type indicate a reference in the text facing the plate.

The Plates

Gavia arctica
BLACK-THROATED DIVER
GAVIIDAE 56 to 69 cm. (body: 36 to 43 cm.)

Their handsome presence and striking summer dress make the divers a glamorous group, for which the North American name 'loon' seems unworthy. Most authorities only recognize 4 species in the order Gaviiformes and all of them occur in Northern Europe, though one is only a very local breeding bird and rare winter visitor to other areas.

Very short tails, solid bones and legs set far back on the body are part of a special adaptation to an aquatic life and make divers ungainly on land. But the Black-throated Diver in full fig is not only the most beautiful member of its select order but perhaps one of the most aesthetically pleasing of all European birds, prompting speculation as to why what has been evolved for the survival of the species should also appeal to the human eye. As with all divers and grebes, the sexes are alike, so that adornment for mutual or communal display must also have a cryptic element to protect the sitting bird. In fact males are slightly larger and thicker-necked than females though this is only relevant when the pair is together. The white-banded area on the scapulars distinguishes this species at once from the Red-throated, and from the Great Northern Diver with its polka-dotted back. But after the moult in the autumn, which involves a flightless period, the position is different; discrimination between the Black-throat and the Great Northern is extremely difficult and B. W. Tucker decided that juveniles of the 2 species were not separable 'at a distance or in poor visibility', conditions often applicable to North European coasts in winter. Adult Black-throats have darker and more uniformly patterned upper parts, their heads and their straight black bills are less massive. These characters are not of much use unless both species are present, but John Parslow notes that in winter the back of the head and neck of the Black-throat are paler than its back whereas both areas on the Great Northern are the same dark shade. Juveniles, which have red-brown eyes, are generally browner and keep much of this plumage into their first full summer, attaining adult dress in the second winter. Legs at all ages are black to grey with flesh-coloured centres to the webs.

The Black-throated Divers of North America are sometimes separated as a species, *G. pacifica*, but it is usual to regard them simply as a race of the one species which breeds more or less round the northern hemisphere, mainly between 60° and 70°N, though extending further north and south in Eurasia, where its range largely overlaps the Red-throat's. It is, however, absent from Greenland, Iceland and Svalbard, where the Red-throat and to some extent the Great Northern appear to occupy its niche. The Black-throat breeds in Scotland (but not in Orkney and Shetland), Scandinavia, and from the mouth of the Oder east into Russia. Its habitat is generally on waters intermediate between the large ones

favoured by the Great Northern and the bare pools and lochans of the Red-throat; the shores may be well vegetated and the surround forest as well as moorland or tundra. The autumn movement is governed by the onset of ice and birds usually winter on coasts directly south of their breeding area. In spring they move north again following the thaw; north Russian birds make a loop migration by way of the Baltic where this takes place relatively early.

In their summer home the first sign of Black-throated Divers is often the rapid quacking call given in flight, very like those of its relatives and not dissimilar from the *ak ak ak* of the female Shelduck. The birds then plane down, sometimes very steeply, to strike the water with their breasts and slide along the surface, wings raised, until momentum is exhausted. They may swim at different levels, partly or almost totally submerging if conscious of danger, and usually dive in the same unobtrusive manner, though at

OPPOSITE *Adult in summer*
BELOW *Adult in winter*

times they spring up and under like a Cormorant. They travel fast under water, sometimes navigating with their wings, and dives up to 5 minutes long and 100 m. deep were recorded by L. Lehtonen. Irene and Alan Joyce watched one bird make 201 dives in just under $3\frac{1}{2}$ hours, with only 3 marked pauses; over half were about 50 seconds long. Fish from fresh or sea water make up about two-thirds of the diet, with the balance of crustaceans, molluscs and worms. Smaller items are swallowed on capture; larger ones are brought to the surface to be 'processed' by the bill.

As well as pairs visiting each other, regular gatherings form throughout the breeding season, even when there are small young, and indulge in 'ritualized threat display' (P. Lindberg). They may also be very noisy, with loud honking and quacking choruses, completely different from the famous diver wail heard on the breeding water. Although they walk with difficulty – their legs down to the ankle joints are contained within the body – divers once airborne fly powerfully, their heads and extended necks held characteristically below the line of the body and legs trailing behind.

The nest, which varies from a bare scrape to a substantial platform of local plant stems, is usually close to the water with one or more access slides, and on an island or headland, sometimes bare, sometimes in quite thick cover. The 2 elongated, olive-brown to umber eggs, with scattered small black spots, are laid from early May in Scotland to mid-June in the far north. They hatch in just over 4 weeks after being incubated from the first egg mainly by the female (Lehtonen). The parents feed the brownish-grey downy chicks for about 5 weeks; they fledge in about 2 months.

Gavia immer
GREAT NORTHERN DIVER

GAVIIDAE 70 to 90 cm. (body: 43 to 50 cm.)

In some ways this is an even more spectacular bird than the Black-throat. Its British common name helps and probably led to *Great Northern* becoming the title of a popular children's book which anticipated by some years the first proved breeding in Britain.

The Great Northern Diver is unmistakable in full plumage; even the partially arrayed non-breeding birds seen during the summer in coastal waters are distinctive. The difficulty of separating it from the Black-throated Diver in winter has been indicated under that species. Typically the Great Northern has a stouter bill, a darker head with more pronounced forehead, and a thicker neck, but there is considerable individual variation. B. W. Tucker notes that traces of summer plumage 'may suffice to settle identity'. The Great Northern can normally be told from the White-billed Diver, *G. adamsii*, by the colour and straightness of the bill, but some birds have pale bills in winter, though the upper ridge remains dark.

Primarily a North American breeding bird, the Great Northern's European footholds are Iceland, Jan Mayen and Bear Islands, with a first Scottish breeding record in 1970. In America the range extends south of the Great Lakes and nearly to 40°N on the west coast. The continental habitat is the larger lake often surrounded by forest and, as K. H. Voous points out, 'characterized by great loneliness and paucity of other bird life'; but in Greenland and Iceland only smaller waters and bare conditions are generally available. Birds move away in autumn before the freeze-up, and become quite common on parts of the British, Irish and French coasts. Their progress north again in spring may be leisurely, and pairs offshore in May long aroused expectation of nesting in Scotland.

Divers show similarity in their habits and actions but the Great Northern is slower than the smaller species to take wing, only succeeding after a prolonged take-off into the wind. Pitching is also a sustained operation, the bird splashing to a stop along the surface. Hence its preference for larger lakes. Once airborne it goes into strong flapping flight with the head-lowered, hunched-back silhouette and webbed feet stretched behind, sole to sole. Rather remarkably for such a heavy, relatively narrow-winged bird, it has a gliding display flight with raised wings which is concerned primarily with pair formation. Mutual displays include neck-up-stretching, wing-arching and rapid dipping of bills in water. There is also a grebe-like display, the birds 'running' over the surface almost upright with bill open and wings beating the water. The 'rolling preen', exposing the white underparts, may be a form of distraction behaviour. A formidable vocabulary of calls has been described, from the *hoo hoo hoo* in flight (G. K. Yeates), the eerie wail with which this species is particularly associated, to 'laughs', 'yodels', and

'noisy outcries'. But in winter, when most European bird-watchers see it, it is usually silent.

Clumsy on land, on which it sometimes uses its wings to help it along, the Great Northern Diver enters another world under water. Then it may travel long distances, sometimes momentarily breaking the surface, and staying below usually for up to a minute in pursuit of the fish which form over half its diet; for the rest it takes crustaceans, marine molluscs and worms. Single birds or pairs may occupy winter feeding territories offshore, and parties may form during the spring moult (there are 2 a year), when they become flightless and vulnerable to oil pollution; most of some 40 birds off the Cornish coast died after the *Torrey Canyon* disaster in 1967 (John Parslow).

OPPOSITE *Adult Great Northern Diver in summer*
ABOVE *Adult Great Northern Diver in winter*

A nest-site is chosen usually close to water but, as the season advances, it may become high and dry. In Iceland little material is used but Canadian nests can be mounds of rotting vegetation. The 2 eggs are laid from the end of May onwards at an interval of at least 48 hours; they are greasy-looking, olive to umber in ground colour with no, few or many black spots and sometimes heavier markings. Incubation by both parents begins with the first egg; the period is about a month. The blackish downy chicks are fed at first by the parents on whose backs they may perch; they feed themselves after about 6 weeks, and fledge at 3 months old.

Gavia adamsii
WHITE-BILLED DIVER
GAVIIDAE 76 to 90 cm.

Slightly larger than the Great Northern Diver, showing an even more pronounced forehead above a big pale yellow bill with an angled lower mandible, the White-billed Diver is sometimes regarded only as a race of *G. immer*, because its range is more or less distinct, stretching from the north of Finland and Novaya Zemlya east along the Siberian coast to Alaska and arctic Canada. But where the 2 overlap in northern Alaska they breed separately and so continue to be treated by most authorities as distinct species. The remarkable bill argues some special adaptation as yet unrevealed. In summer the White-billed has a slightly darker head and the white stripes on the neck are fewer but thicker (B. L. Sage). In winter the bill remains the best distinguishing character.

Apart from the Finnish toehold, this species is known as a rare winter visitor or vagrant to Northern Europe but has been recorded more frequently in British waters in recent years. Its habits are similar to those of the Great Northern; it feeds almost entirely on fish, diving on average for over a minute (Sage).

27

Gavia stellata
RED-THROATED DIVER
GAVIIDAE 56 to 58 cm. (body: 36 cm.)

The smallest of the divers is also the most numerous and widely distributed. Almost as big as the Black-throat, it can be distinguished at quite long range by the uptilted appearance of the rather thin bill, due to the angled lower mandible. In summer the upper parts are lighter than those of the other species, but the red throat patch is not a very good character in the field, as it looks almost black at a distance. When a pair is seen together, the male has the thicker neck and head. In winter the upper parts are grey, finely spotted with white, and show up the white of the under parts, which extends up the neck to the face. Immature birds are, however, generally browner above and less pure white below, so the bill remains the best distinguishing mark. As with other divers, some individuals may show enough of the breeding plumage at any season to clinch identification.

The breeding distribution overlaps those of all the other divers, but lies mainly between 60° and 80°N. In Northern Europe Donegal in Ireland is the most southerly station and Svalbard the most arctic; Iceland, much of Scotland and its isles, Scandinavia, the Baltic shores, the northern archipelagos and European Russia are all included, with some evidence of a southward extension in recent years. In autumn the birds retreat before the oncoming ice and, while many winter on the edge of the summer range, others reach the Mediterranean and also occur on in-

('cuddies') and, in fresh water, trout, char and several coarse fish. Molluscs, crustaceans, large insects, even frogs and some plant material are also recorded in the diet. After feeding, the Red-throat, like many fish-eaters, may sip water. It takes off more easily than other divers, sometimes even from land, but finds difficulty if there is a strong wind behind it, so that it can be 'cornered' on a small pool. In the air it has the same powerful beating flight as its relatives and the hunchback silhouette. It walks with difficulty in semi-erect posture, resting every few yards.

This is perhaps the most sociable of the divers, sometimes breeding in colonial groups and forming loose flocks on the sea in winter. Early in the season there is an aerial gliding display, as with the Great Northern Diver, probably as the male introduces the female to his territory. On small waters visits take place between pairs and some displays are performed by several birds in concert. Julian Huxley defined the 'plesiosaur race' between 2 to 4 birds, who swim for some way 'with hinder half of body submerged, neck upwards and forwards in stiff position, head and beak inclined somewhat forward', then swirl round and retrace their course. This display starts early and continues even after the young are hatched, stimulated by the appearance of other adults. Before mating, the female may dive and reappear slowly, with head bent down, to be joined by the male, who patters over the water to meet her. After the pair has formed, the 'snake ceremony' indicates intense excitement: one bird swims behind the other, both with necks arched and bills wide open, though with the tips

OPPOSITE *Adult in summer*
BELOW *Adult in winter*

land waters. The largest number in a British estuary in 1972-3 was 29 in the Essex Blackwater.

On the water the Red-throat shows the almost tailless outline of the family but often swims partly submerged, sinking quietly beneath the surface if alarmed, though it also dives with a spring, perhaps to gain greater depth. Propulsion under water is normally by the webbed feet but several observers have seen the wings brought into play. Dives may last up to 1½ minutes and take the bird 9 m. down to hunt small fish; sprats, herrings, sand-eels, flounders, coal-fish

of the mandibles in the water. This is accompanied by Huxley's 'rolling growl' note. Actual coition takes place on shore, the male standing almost upright on his mate's back. Various other actions have been described and, accepting that divers are not very closely related to grebes, the similarity of some of their displays could be due to convergent evolution in the same environment.

The divers' usual *kwuck kwuck kwuck . . . ,* so evocative of the wilderness when heard high overhead, and the mournful wail on the water – sometimes uttered in winter – are well-known

28

Red-throat calls. The *kwuck* may be doubled and repeated with mounting excitement, and E. M. Nicholson also noted a noisy 'courtship chorus', which seems to relate to the 'rolling growl'. Other calls have been verbalized, almost as diversely as the observers concerned.

An island or the bank of a small pool are favourite nest-sites and, although it can waddle quite well on land, the Red-throat usually breeds close to the water, with one or more slides by which the sitting bird can leave and submerge unobtrusively. The nest may be rudimentary or substantial; the (usually) 2 eggs are laid from mid-May in the south to June in the north of the range and are oily-looking, yellowish-olive to umber with rather sparse black spots and blotches. The female takes the greater share of incubation, which may last for 4 weeks. The greyish downy young are then tended, often communally, for about a month, the parents flying from small nesting waters to fish for them in larger lakes or the sea; they fly when about 6 weeks old. When quite small chicks have been known to crawl over 100 m. through woodland to join the parents on another water (C. von Braun, A. C. Hessle, S. Sjölander).

Podiceps cristatus
GREAT CRESTED GREBE
PODICIPITIDAE 48 cm. (body: 30 cm.)

A number of anatomical differences separate grebes from divers, the most obvious being their lobed but only partially webbed toes, whereas the divers' 3 front toes are completely webbed. Resemblances such as the reduced tail and the setting back of the legs are no doubt adaptations to an aquatic life.

The breeding distribution of the Great Crested Grebe is curiously discontinuous. The largest area is a broad band across Eurasia from western Europe to the Pacific at about 40°N and to below 30° in south China. The second area is in Africa south of the Sahara, excluding the great forests and deserts; the third is in south-western and south-eastern Australia, Tasmania and New Zealand. The European breeding habitat is on still waters varying in size but essentially with fringing vegetation of reeds and other tall aquatic plants. Slow-flowing rivers may qualify and the most northerly outposts are by the near-fresh and tideless Gulf of Bothnia. In autumn these and other northern areas are abandoned and there is in general a movement south and west to sheltered offshore waters, where quite large wintering flocks may build up, including birds from frozen inland lakes. The largest number in a British estuary in 1972-3 was 352 in the Firth of Forth.

The Great Crested Grebe is one of the most strikingly adorned of the family, using its ruff or tippet in display as Raymond Watson shows. This splendid appearance and especially the silky white under parts nearly caused its extinction in the days of ornate human millinery; bird protection in Britain really got under way with the campaign to save this species from exploitation. Although unmistakable in summer, in winter the Great Crested can be confused with the slightly smaller Red-necked Grebe; distinctions between them are discussed on plate five.

The dark and light stripes of the downy chick are retained on the head of the juvenile, illustrated, whose body resembles an adult in winter. In the succeeding immature plumage the ear-tufts are already discernible. Adults in winter show traces of the tippet. In all plumages the thin neck distinguishes grebes from divers. The bill is also thinner and sharper-looking. In flight the Great Crested has been described graphically but somewhat inaccurately as a jet-propelled pencil. It certainly looks attenuated, but the eye-catching feature is the broad white bars on the rapidly beating wings; these are almost completely hidden when at rest. The legs trail behind and the hump-backed silhouette recalls a diver or a saw-billed duck such as a Goosander or Merganser.

Although it keeps low in the water, a Great Crested Grebe in full sail with neck held erect is impressive; when at rest it becomes a rounded lump, its head tucked into the neck feathers; then it rolls over to preen and shows the white under parts like a transformation scene. On land

it is clumsy and splay-footed. When moved to fly, which it does reluctantly, it takes off with a pattering run along the surface, pitching back breast-foremost. Like a diver it may submerge quietly or with a forward leap. Underwater the feet propel it after small fish of many species both in fresh and salt water. Dives are usually fairly shallow (2 to 4 m.) and last about half a minute. A good proportion of the diet in summer consists of large insects, such as mayflies and dragonflies, and their larvae, crustaceans, molluscs, occasional newts and tadpoles and some plant material. Like other grebes it swallows its own feathers and feeds them to the

OPPOSITE *Two summer adults in foreground and a juvenile behind*
BELOW *Adult in winter*

young, apparently to blanket the sharp edges of inedible stomach contents.

The Great Crested Grebe begins its rituals by 'advertising' for a mate with a special posture and croaking call (K. E. L. Simmons). The extensive mutual displays were the subject of a pioneer behaviour study by Julian Huxley. The commonest form is head-shaking, when the pair swims together, raise eartufts and ruff, and shake their heads at each other, now fast, now slowly. Another bizarre performance is the 'penguin dance', in which the birds, after diving for billfuls of weed, come together breast to breast

right out of the water, teeter for a few seconds, then relax. These and other actions are accompanied by a repertoire of calls from a shrill bark to a noise like a dentist's drill. But the sound most associated with the nesting season is the ceaseless *pee-a pee-a* of the food-begging chicks.

Great Crested Grebes are usually strongly territorial, but in some areas quite large colonies may form, apparently where the feeding is very rich. The season may also be protracted, with first eggs in January in Britain; but in some years, if vegetation is sparse, pairs do not breed at all. The nest, a mass of wet vegetation anchored to living plants, may be conspicuous or well-hidden. The chalky white eggs, rather pointed at both ends, are laid in a central depression and become deeply stained as the sitting bird normally covers them on leaving the nest. The usual clutch is 3 to 5, incubated by the parents in turn from the first egg and hatching in about 4 weeks. The chicks, active at once, habitually perch on the backs of the adults, who often divide the brood between them. They become more or less independent in 6 weeks if they survive the attentions of pike and other enemies. There is sometimes a second brood.

Podiceps grisegena
RED-NECKED GREBE
PODICIPITIDAE 43 cm. (body: 25 cm.)

Most wild animals impress the observer with the perfection of their proportions. There are a few exceptions, for example the hyenas among mammals, and this species, which breeds discontinuously right round the northern hemisphere – it is sometimes called Holboell's Grebe in North America – among birds; its topheavy appearance is one of its field characters.

The European race *grisegena* breeds in the centre and north (to 65°N in Sweden) of the continent, with an extension into Asia (the upper catchment area of the River Ob); it nests sporadically in the Netherlands, and in Asia Minor. The race *holboelli* breeds over a large area of eastern Asia based on the Sea of Okhotsk, and in North America from Alaska in a broad belt south-east to the Great Lakes and sporadically beyond. The European breeding habitat is on inland waters from small pools to large lakes, normally with thick vegetation both under water and round the banks. K. H. Voous comments that competition with the Great Crested Grebe is likely in the large central area where they overlap, but in the pools of the northern taiga and shrub tundra this species has only the Slavonian Grebe as rival. There is a general movement in autumn to the south and west; much of the European breeding range is abandoned and birds winter round the Baltic and North Sea coasts. A few reach the north and eastern Mediterranean; more favour the Black Sea and, especially, the Caspian Sea. Generally, sheltered shores and estuaries are its preferred haunts.

There should be no difficulty in identifying a Red-necked Grebe in summer and useful traces of the plumage may be retained for most of the year. In winter the curious thick-necked appearance already mentioned helps to separate it even at a distance from the Great Crested; also the outline of the head becomes rounded, whereas the larger species continues to sport rudimentary eartufts. At closer range, the Red-necked is seen to lack the white stripe over the eye and the cheeks are greyish, paling to white on the throat; the Great Crested is more cleanly black and white. But its pink bill at all ages is a much better character; the Red-necked has a relatively stouter organ, the upper mandible mainly black with a yellow cutting edge; the lower mandible distally black and yellow at the base. Although duller in winter, the yellow should still be visible. This species also has a greyish neck and grey mottling on the breast; these distinctions, with its size, silhouette and bill colour should separate it from the smaller grebes. In flight it shows a similar black and white wing pattern to the Great Crested.

Juveniles are rather similar to washed-out summer adults, with a reddish tint to the neck, brownish upper parts and striped and mottled head pattern; the wing bar is also somewhat obscured with brown. But when the first winter moult is complete something very like the adult

state is attained. The Red-necked Grebe sometimes swims in the open with head erect, sometimes keeps to cover. It moves on land more easily than other grebes and takes off into flight with the same pattering run. The diet, both in fresh water and the sea, is largely of fish up to

OPPOSITE *Adult in summer*
BELOW *Adult in winter*

15 cm. long; these are hunted under water in dives lasting up to a minute (but usually very much shorter), during which the wings are occasionally used as well as the feet. Small reptiles and amphibians, crustaceans and molluscs are also eaten and, in summer, a number of bugs, beetles, dragonflies and their larvae. Some plant material is taken and there is the usual grebe ingestion of feathers.

The displays of the Red-necked Grebe resemble those of the Great Crested Grebe, from 'advertising' with erected eartufts to head-shaking, the penguin dance with weed carrying

and 'bouncy dives, from which the bird emerges with the head low over the back, the bill forward, the breast puffed out and raised, the tail cocked and the end of the body low in the water' (B. L. Sage). On arrival at the breeding water there are noisy communal displays by night. The song, according to Sage, is 'a long-drawn wailing or whinnying, somewhat nasal in quality at first and quavering towards the end'. Both sexes may sing and then swim round each other, uttering a repeated *keck*, which is also the usual call. Outside the breeding season the Red-necked Grebe tends, like the divers, to be silent.

The nest-site is similar to that of the Great Crested Grebe; so is the nest of piled-up water plants on which, as with other grebes, mating takes place. The 4 to 5 chalky white eggs (larger clutches are recorded in America) are laid in Europe from the end of April onwards and soon become stained and scratched. Incubation by both sexes begins probably with the first egg and lasts about 23 days, after which the parents tend the active striped young for at least 2 months, feeding them at first on insect larvae, then on progressively larger fish. There is only a single brood.

Podiceps auritus
SLAVONIAN GREBE
PODICIPITIDAE 33 cm. (body: 20 cm.)

This is another northern hemisphere species, with the alternative American name of Horned Grebe; the British epithet is picturesque rather than descriptive of the bird's origins. The Slavonian definitely belongs to the colourful section of the family and the compelling red eye has gazed out of many a bird-photographer's portrait of it 'at home' on the nest.

In its breeding distribution the Slavonian rivals the Red-necked as the most northerly grebe. Their American ranges are very similar but, coming east, the Slavonian is the only grebe nesting in Iceland, quite commonly in suitable habitats; it has bred in the Faeroe Islands and is established at a few localities in the north of Scotland, to which the Red-necked is only a winter visitor. Local in Norway and Sweden, where it is more widespread than its relative, it is absent from Denmark and Germany, but then breeds right across Eurasia, mainly between 50° and 60°N, to terminate in an area round the Sea of Okhotsk rather like that of the Red-necked Grebe. Like it too, it vacates most of the summer range in autumn and has much the same coastal wintering areas, extending further south-west but being absent from most of the eastern Medi-

though B. W. Tucker enters a caveat about probably young Slavonians having bills almost as slender as Black-necked Grebes 'with minimum tilt'. Both species show clearly black and white in winter as compared with the dull browns of the Little Grebe, but the Slavonian's dark crown ends at the eye and the white cheek patches almost meet at the nape. They are more restricted on the Black-necked, though again Tucker warns of individual variation. The Slavonian also has a smaller white wing-bar (secondary flight feathers only), is slightly larger, and usually holds its head up when swimming; the Black-necked Grebe appears rather dumpier. Juvenile Slavonians have a less defined black and white pattern than the adults, browner-looking and with dusky cheeks.

Whereas the Black-necked Grebe tends to conceal itself at its breeding stations, this species is easier to see, though it sinks in the water if suspicious; it is said to take wing, with the usual laboured grebe take-off and landing, more readily, and to dive less, with a preference for a forward spring when it does. Small fish, molluscs and crustaceans are staple food, with various insects (caddis flies, true flies and beetles) and their larvae in summer. Some plants are eaten and quantities of feathers swallowed, forming up to two-thirds of the contents of some stomachs.

OPPOSITE *Adult in summer*
BELOW *Adult in winter*

terranean. The preferred breeding habitat is a quiet pool or slow-flowing peaty river with a good growth of sedges, mare's-tails and other emergent aquatic plants. In winter a sea loch, fjord or sheltered shore is favoured and inland waters are frequently occupied. At this time Slavonians are usually solitary in Europe, but in America quite large flocks may form.

Confusion with the Black-necked Grebe in summer should only occur at a distance or in poor visibility; not only the neck colour but the placing of the eartufts are different. The bills are the best distinguishing characters at all seasons,

In display mutual head-shaking and the penguin dance appear again, with variations, and the male has been photographed on the water by Eric Hosking with neck stretched out and eartufts raised; a similar attitude may be taken up on the nest as the mate approaches, suggesting the element of hostility which behaviour students believe is never far below the threshold in mated life. Great excitement also precedes coition on the nest. Some displays are accompanied by a low-pitched but penetrating rippling call, rather like the trill of the Little Grebe, and a number of remarkable notes have been de-

scribed to fit different breeding season situations. The usual contact call seems to be a repeated *uck*. Begging chicks keep up an incessant *pee-a pee-a*.

Slavonian Grebes are faithful to their breeding stations, returning even to the same few square metres year after year. They may either nest solitarily or, if conditions are congenial, in loose colonies though less regularly than Black-necked Grebes. The nest is sometimes quite exposed, but usually well concealed in sedges or other lacustrine plants and is the typical grebe mound of wet vegetation, built up in shallow water or floating and anchored. Material may be added during the incubation period, which lasts between 22 and 25 days, starting with the third or fourth egg of the clutch, usually of 3 to 6 eggs. These are chalky-white and double-pointed, but soon stain to become quite orange-red. The female does most of the incubating, but both parents generally tend the striped young, which frequently settle on their backs in the early days of the fledging period. Later one parent, presumed to be the male, may desert the family. A second brood follows occasionally in favourable seasons.

Podiceps nigricollis
BLACK-NECKED GREBE
PODICIPITIDAE 30 cm. (body: 18 cm.)

This species shares with the Red-throated and White-billed Divers the distinguishing feature of a 'tiptilted' bill, an effect due to the angling of the lower mandible. It is remarkable that a character which, though obvious in the hand, does not seem so decisive, should show up in the field at considerable distances and determine identification.

Like the Great Crested Grebe, the Black-necked has a discontinuous breeding distribution. Their Eurasian ranges are somewhat similar but this species covers less of western Europe, little of Scandinavia and, to the east, cuts off somewhere near Lake Baikal, leaving a separate enclave round the Sea of Okhotsk. In Africa it is likewise more restricted than the larger species. Known as the Eared Grebe in North America, it occupies a rather irregular block of country in the western half of that continent.

This curious distribution includes many different major habitats. There have been fairly recent spreads northward in America and westward in Europe, where lately a decline has followed and this is now a very rare breeding species in Britain and Ireland. The favoured habitats are shallow lakes, marshes and brackish lagoons with a lush underwater vegetation and plenty of littoral cover. In winter the Black-necked Grebe retreats southward but remains, unlike its relatives, mainly inland, though found on estuaries and coastal waters.

Its discrimination from the Slavonian Grebe

North America.

This is the most regularly colonial of the European grebes and it often nests amid colonies of gulls and terns, unmolested and apparently deriving protection from their noisy presence. The nest is much smaller than the Slavonian Grebe's and can be built in a few hours. It is usually well hidden in dense vegetation. The 3 to 5 initially chalky white eggs, laid from mid-April in continental Europe, are incubated from the first egg by both sexes and hatch in about 3 weeks. Both parents tend the striped young for an as yet undetermined fledging period. There is sometimes a second brood.

Tachybaptus ruficollis
LITTLE GREBE or DABCHICK
PODICIPITIDAE 27 cm. (body: 15 cm.)

Widespread in the Old World, the tubby Dabchick is now usually put in a separate genus from the other European grebes. Its breeding range covers most of western Europe south of 60°N and bounded by a line from the Gulf of Riga to the Caspian Sea, south of which it extends through Iran to the Himalayan region and India, and on to South-east Asia, east China and Japan. The African distribution covers the continent south of the Sahara, with some enclaves close to the Mediterranean. Related species occur in much of America and Australasia. The breeding habitat includes pools, permanent marshes and slow-flowing streams, usually characterized by lush plant growth above and below the surface.

OPPOSITE *Adult Black-necked Grebe in summer*
BELOW *Winter adults of Little Grebe (left) and Black-necked Grebe adult (right)*

has been discussed under that species. The juvenile resembles the winter adult but shows less definition between the dark crown and lighter cheeks. In its general habits it resembles the Slavonian Grebe but is usually unobtrusive when nesting. Dives last about half a minute, during which it hunts mainly aquatic larvae, small molluscs and crustaceans; when swimming on the surface it snaps up insects deftly. The usual calls are a quiet *pee-eep*, a sharp alarm note and the 'song', a repeated rippling *bidder vidder*. At least 6 mutual displays have been described, including forms of head-shaking and the penguin dance, by Nancy McAllister in

Areas likely to be ice-bound are left in winter and there is a fairly general move coastwards in autumn.

This is superficially the least adorned European grebe but the glossy dark brown breeding plumage is not unattractive; the rich chestnut of face and foreneck contrasts with the patch of yellow-green skin at the base of the bill, which is black with a whitish tip. The legs are mainly dark or dull green and the eye is red-brown. The underparts are pale and silky. In winter the chestnut on the head is lost and the whole plumage is generally a lighter brown. Juveniles are darker than winter adults, with streaked heads,

but first winter birds are even lighter coloured.

The Dabchick is relatively mobile on its rare visits to the land, but its element is the water where it submerges both quietly·or with a leap, staying under for only about 15 seconds. The food is the common grebe mixture of fish, very small in this case, molluscs, crustaceans and insects both adult and larval, with a little vegetable matter. Feathers are not swallowed as readily as by other grebes.

In winter Little Grebes may be found singly, in small parties or even in flocks; but when breeding they are territorial. The loud trilling call is then the main indication of their presence; duets are the chief form of mutual display, replacing the visual stimuli of the more adorned species. The long breeding season is from March until September. The nest is often made of dead leaves as well as of water plants, but is of usual grebe type and generally quite well concealed. The clutch of 4 to 6 chalky white eggs is incubated by both parents in turn for 19 to 20 days. The attractively striped chicks are active at once, tended by both parents, and fly when 6 to 7 weeks old. There are 2, sometimes 3 broods in a season.

Fulmarus glacialis
FULMAR
PROCELLARIIDAE 47 cm.

The Fulmar 'flying free' has in the past century been transformed from a comparative rarity in all but the most northerly European waters to one of the more familiar sea birds, at least round the coasts of Britain, Ireland and northern France. Its name means 'foul gull', an allusion to its habit of ejecting rancid oil when threatened, and at first sight it looks like a stiff-winged Herring Gull. But the heavier head, short thick neck and deep-set dark eyes soon distinguish it and, at closer range, the external nostrils reveal its relationship to other 'tube-noses': petrels, shearwaters and albatrosses. A gull-like character is the contrast between the light grey back and upper wing surfaces (which have no black tips) and the white or yellow-tinged head, body and rather fanned tail. But there is a more or less uniform grey to brown plumage phase which becomes progressively commoner with increasing latitude until it makes up over half of some arctic breeding populations. The evolutionary cause behind this gradation is as obscure as that governing the bridled form of Common Guillemot. The Fulmar's legs vary from yellowish to bluish flesh colour; the bill, also variable, usually has a yellowish tip and dark 'tubes'. After moulting their 2 fluffy down plumages, juveniles are almost impossible to tell from adults in the field.

The Fulmar is now split into 3 races. The large-billed *auduboni*, which has spread so remarkably, has its numerical strongholds in Iceland, the Faeroe Islands, northern Scotland and its islands. To the north of it the small-billed *glacialis* breeds in the European arctic archipelagos, Greenland and arctic Canada in scattered colonies. The North Pacific race *rodgersii* has an equally 'spotty' distribution. Some authorities regard the Antarctic Fulmar *F. glacialoides* as a fourth race: certainly it is very closely related to the northern Fulmar. The large-billed race also nests locally in Norway and, having completed its encirclement of Britain and Ireland, now breeds in Brittany and Jersey (1975). This expansion began about 1878, when St Kilda was the only breeding station in the British area, and there has been much argument about the reason for it; on one view it is due to the expansion of the trawling fleets, which provide an almost perennial supply of fish offal, but Fulmars are known to have scavenged on the whalers of the seventeenth century. Another argument is that a special genotype with a proclivity to spread in small colonies evolved in Iceland. Thirdly it might be due to the warming up of the eastern North Atlantic. The debate continues.

Non-breeding Fulmars are wandering the oceans at all times, and in winter the small-billed race moves southward in front of the ice. British-ringed birds have reached Spain, crossed the Atlantic and have entered the Barents Sea east of Svalbard. Actually the colonies are only deserted for a couple of months between the fledging of the last young in September and November or December when the adults re-appear at them, though they leave again if the weather turns bad.

The occupation of the ledges is accompanied by noisy cackling from one, 2 or more birds and this continues throughout the season, even the nearly fledged juveniles joining in at times. These mutual displays and greeting ceremonies consist of various head and neck movements, some quite contortional; and fights with interlocked bills also take place. Fulmars display and call on the water as well.

In contrast to the hubbub on the ledges, on the wing Fulmars are usually silent; they may pass apparently for hours backwards and forwards close to the cliff-top, following its indentations as they glide along with intermittent bursts of flapping to restore momentum. They also plane low over the sea like shearwaters and frequently settle, pattering over the surface to take off again. On land they rest on their shanks and walk clumsily.

Originally the Fulmar's diet was probably mainly surface plankton, as it is seldom seen to dive, supplemented by 'natural' carrion, before man came on the scene with his whalers and fishing boats. Huge flocks may gather round one of these and the birds are as clamorous as gulls as they compete for the fat, offal or whole fish. They still scoop up plankton, especially when feeding young.

Although typically nesting in colonies on rather broad, often well-vegetated ledges, Fulmars in their rapid expansion have taken to steep banks, talus slopes and scree, sand dunes, beaches, ruins and even occupied dwellings as well as flat ground. Recently they have been seen at nests of the Rook *Corvus frugilegus* in trees in Scotland but not yet proved to lay in them. Inland cliffs and quarries are occupied, sometimes miles from the sea. The nest site is usually fairly open and, if the ground allows it, a scrape is formed but not lined, though occasionally framed with pebbles. Two weeks before laying, the birds temporarily and mysteriously disappear. Then, about the beginning of May in the south, they return and the (normally) single white egg is laid, to be incubated by both parents in alternating spells of 4 to 5 days; it hatches at anything between 41 and 57 days. The downy chick is fed by regurgitation once or twice a day and fledges in about 7 weeks; the parents stop feeding it several days before its first flight, when it weighs more than an adult. After spending 3 or 4 years at sea, young Fulmars start prospecting nest-sites but do not breed until about 7 years old, with an expectation of 9 more years of active life.

The Operation Seafarer figure for the British and Irish Fulmar breeding population in 1969–70 was some 305,000 occupied sites, making it one of the most numerous sea birds; the north-west of Scotland with Shetland, Orkney and the Outer Hebrides (which include St Kilda) accounted for 88 per cent of the total. No conservation problems have yet reared their heads alongside this successful colonist.

Adult and nestling

Puffinus puffinus
MANX SHEARWATER
PROCELLARIIDAE 36 cm.

A scientific name reminiscent of a different bird, a geographical adjective which for long did not apply, as it deserted the Isle of Man, but an apt descriptive noun are man's adornments of one of the most studied North European sea birds. The only black and white shearwater likely to be seen in the area (the Little Shearwater, *P. assimilis*, is a very rare visitor) is the typical race *puffinus*. At close range the hook-tipped bill and pinkish webs on the dark feet are notable; in general the bird has a deceptively soft appearance for such a hardy ocean traveller. Juveniles are indistinguishable from adults.

Only the typical race breeds in Northern Europe, from Iceland, the Faeroe Islands, Britain and Ireland (its main strongholds) to Brittany in France. In autumn birds disperse across the Atlantic and may winter mainly off eastern South America, though some birds reach Australian waters. The Balearic race *mauretanicus*, which is quite distinctive, being more or less uniformly brown, occasionally comes to northern waters between June and November.

In daytime Manx Shearwaters are only seen at sea, either 'doing their thing' over it as they tilt from side to side, now black, now white, with occasional bouts of flapping; or settled, sometimes in huge 'rafts', when they allow a close approach before duck-diving with wings half spread. Silent by day, they become daemonic voices on overcast nights as they fly over their nesting burrows, exchanging wild roo-kooing calls with their mates below. Quieter sounds are heard in the burrows, where there are mutual displays; pairs re-mate annually. The main food is small fish, caught when hovering low over the

begins at the end of April in the south, a single dull white egg which soon becomes stained. It hatches after 7½ weeks, during which the parents incubate it in turns usually of 3 to 5 days.

The downy chick is fed by regurgitation about 2 nights out of 3, eventually becoming twice as heavy as its parents, who desert it after 7 or 8 weeks. It takes off for the sea when about 10 weeks old, much at risk to large gulls. After wandering for a couple of years, the survivors return home but do not breed until 5 years old. Their remarkable homing capacity has been tested by releasing ringed birds right outside their normal range; one returned to Wales from Boston, U.S., in 12½ days.

Operation Seafarer found this a very hard bird to count: the estimate for Britain and Ireland was 'almost certainly over 175,000 pairs' and possibly over 300,000; there is insufficient evidence to suggest any major trend in numbers.

Puffinus gravis
GREAT SHEARWATER
PROCELLARIIDAE 43 to 46 cm.

Breeding mainly in the Tristan da Cunha group, numbers of this southern species visit the North Atlantic from June to October. The upper surface is brown, with darker wings and tail (the base of which shows a white patch) and a conspicuous black cap. The white under parts may have numerous dark flecks; the white of the throat, almost surrounding the neck, emphasizes the dark crown. When moulting, a white band is exposed along the wing. Juveniles are indistinguishable. The flight consists of very long glides and spells of flapping, often low over the waves which the bird may patter with its dark feet. It

OPPOSITE *Adult Manx Shearwater*
BELOW *Great Shearwater adult (left) and Sooty Shearwater adult (right)*

water or by shallow dives. Some offal may be taken and remains of molluscs have been identified in stomachs.

Except when gale-driven, Manx Shearwaters only land to breed, excavating or occupying burrows on turf-capped islands and headlands or scree slopes and hill tops up to 600 m. The workings, along which the birds pad on their shanks, may be from 0·5 to 2 m. deep, with a sparsely lined nest chamber at the end, and frequently inter-communicate. Like Fulmars, the birds disappear for about 10 days before laying, apparently to stoke up for the vigils ahead. Laying

feeds on squids, fishing offal and small fish, taking them from the surface or by diving. Flocks may build up and follow boats and whales. When satiated, the birds rest at sea, bathing and preening.

Puffinus griseus
SOOTY SHEARWATER
PROCELLARIIDAE 40 cm.

This almost uniformly dark-plumaged species is another refugee from the southern winter, as it

breeds on Australasian and South American coasts. A pale line shows along the coverts of the underwing; otherwise the bird earns its descriptive name; bill and legs are also blackish. It is most likely to be seen offshore from July to September, chiefly on the western coasts of Ireland and Britain, extending up to southern Norway. Often seen with Great Shearwaters, it resembles them in many ways but has a faster wing-beat. It feeds largely on squids, diving after them and swimming under water with the aid of its wings.

Cory's Shearwater, *Calonectris diomedea*, is marginally larger than the Great Shearwater from which it differs in being grey-brown above and whitish below, merging with the upper parts on head and neck. There is often a white area at the base of the tail and the yellowish bill can be seen when close-up. At a distance the wings look more bowed and angular than those of other shearwaters and the flight is 'somewhat lackadaisical' (R. Prytherch). Breeding in the Mediterranean area and the Atlantic islands, it is seen off France, south-west England and Ireland usually from July to September, sometimes in parties.

Hydrobates pelagicus
STORM PETREL
HYDROBATIDAE 16·5 cm.

Apparently tripping over the water like the saint from which the petrels derive their name, the 'stormie' has a wealth of nautical lore behind it. Bird-watchers often liken it to a House Martin, *Delichon urbica*, but this is purely superficial because the petrel is blackish-brown all over, including legs, bill and eyes, except for the white rump, a little white under the wing and, in mint plumage, a narrow white wing-bar. It is the smallest European sea bird.

The world breeding range is confined to the North Atlantic, from Iceland, Norway (Lofoten Islands), the Faeroe Islands, Britain, Ireland, the Channel Isles, France, Iberia, to the Canary Islands and the western Mediterranean. But the population moves a long way to winter probably off the southern tip of Africa. Ringing has also revealed some interchange between breeding colonies. Sometimes migrating birds are driven inland by gales in great numbers, almost all to perish.

Storm Petrels traditionally dance in the wake of ships, but less regularly than Wilson's Petrel, *Oceanites oceanicus*, of the Antarctic, a very rare visitor to Europe and much more like St Peter in its 'walking'. The Storm Petrel spends the day at sea, unless in its burrow, searching for the zooplankton and small fish which it plucks out of the water with its bill.

At night, whether moonlit or cloudy, it dares to approach the land and may become noisy, calling a loud *terr-chick* (P. Davis) in its courtship chases. Davis also discovered that the famous churring or purring with its interjectory hiccups – 'like a fairy being sick' (C. Oldham) – issues mainly from single birds and has the same functions as passerine song: to announce territorial ownership and to attract a mate. Mated pairs call *terr-chick* under ground and various other affectionate noises have been described. All petrels rest and shuffle about on their shanks; coming into the open, the Storm Petrel keeps on its toes by fluttering its wings and takes off easily.

Several pairs may share the same entrance to their burrows, which acquire a characteristic musty smell. They are excavated in the turf caps of islands and headlands at about 30 cm. a day, the earth scraped downward by the bill and then thrown backwards by the feet. An average length is 75 cm., but some are only several centimetres deep; some burrows are offshoots of shearwater, Puffin or rabbit holes. Storm or boulder-covered beaches and rock crevices, including the interstices of stone walls, are also extensively used and may contain substantial pad nests (R. F. Ruttledge); in earth there is usually only a round scrape. The pre-laying occupation of the nest-site averages 6 to 7 weeks and the single roundish, red-spotted white egg is laid from the end of May

onwards in south Wales. It hatches after about 40 days incubation by both parents in equal 3-day stints. The silver-grey downy chick is brooded for the first week of its 9-week fledging period and mainly fed by night from the parents' throats. Feeds fall off as the fledgling doubles the adult's weight. For several nights it exercises its wings outside the burrow, then takes off on its own, a replica of the adult.

A census of petrel colonies presents enormous difficulties. During Operation Seafarer in 1969-70 over 60 known breeding stations in Britain, Ireland and the Channel Islands were visited; 2 Irish colonies were estimated to hold at least 10,000 pairs each; 6 others were given 1000 or more pairs.

Oceanodroma leucorrhoa
LEACH'S PETREL
HYDROBATIDAE 20 cm.

Since it seldom follows ships and is nocturnal on land, this is one of the least known of the abundant North Atlantic sea birds. Larger and browner-looking than the Storm and Wilson's Petrels, its upper parts have a bluish bloom, contrasting with the light band on the wing coverts and the rather paler under parts. The forked tail and the dark central feathers of the white rump are not good field characters except at close range, but the wings look relatively long (span up to 48 cm.) and tern-like. Juveniles are not distinguishable from adults. The best means of identification is by the 'buoyant, erratic flight' (B. W. Tucker).

Although the North European breeding stations are few and small – Iceland (Westman Islands), the Faeroe Islands, 5 off Scotland, possibly Lofoten Islands and western Ireland – the east North American colonies, some on wooded islands, are enormous and the Newfoundland population is estimated in millions. Four other races breed on either side of the North Pacific. European birds are believed to winter, like Storm Petrels, in the tropics off South Africa. This species suffers even more catastrophic 'wrecks' than its relative. In autumn 1952 nearly 7000 were found in Britain and Ireland and some reached Switzerland.

Leach's Petrel often settles briefly on the water, from which most of its sustenance comes: zooplankton, small fish, the excrement of marine mammals and offal. Most of its feeding takes place at night and J. A. Ainslie and R. Atkinson described 2 kinds of nocturnal flight, one purposeful and suggesting the birds might be taking moths, the other erratic, probably a display, accompanied by calling before the birds shuffled to their burrows. A staccato ticking call ending in a slurred trill is given both in flight and underground, where there is also a musical, whirring, crooning song.

European nest-sites are similar to those of the Storm Petrel, in excavated burrows or rock

crevices. The nest scrape is usually lined and a single white egg laid in it at the end of May in Scotland. This hatches after about 7 weeks shared incubation and the chick is fed for another 9 or 10 weeks before it is left to fledge on its own. The known British breeding stations were all visited during Operation Seafarer in 1969–70 but it was not possible to arrive at a population figure; at a guess, some hundreds of pairs.

Adult Leach's Petrel (left)
and adult Storm Petrel (right)

Sula bassana
GANNET
SULIDAE 90 cm. (body: 58 cm.)

With a wing-span of almost 2 m. this is the largest North European sea bird; the adult (lowest bird and close-up head on the plate) is unmistakable even at long range, its plumage shining white when the black wing tips cannot be seen. But juveniles and immatures cause trouble, even masking the characteristic torpedo outline and pointed tail, and prompting thoughts of albatrosses. The juvenile plumage (top bird) is spangled brown, from which there is a gradual transition over the next 4 years to the gleaming adult; the bird second from the top of the plate shows the second year phase. J. B. Nelson has pointed out that the greenish lines on the toes are yellower on the male, more turquoise on the female, a useful character for close-up observations.

Although some authorities suggest that the South African *S. capensis* and Australasian *S. serrator* are conspecific with it, it is usual to regard *S. bassana* as confined to the North Atlantic, breeding in Newfoundland and the Gulf of St Lawrence, Iceland, the Faeroe Islands, Norway, Britain, Ireland, the Channel Isles and Brittany, with a world population estimated at 200,000 pairs; numbers and stations are still increasing. The Gannet is a partial migrant; in their first year birds reach West Africa and the Mediterranean. Older birds winter off Iberia and the Bay of Biscay; adults disperse round their colonies, which are tenanted for much of the year.

The Gannet's usual flight is a mixture of rather rapid beats and glides at some height, but it often comes low, planing and swerving over the waves; at other times it climbs and soars. Frequently solitary, gannets may travel in small parties, adults and immatures mixed. Their most spectacular action is the plunge dive from over 30 m. up, at first with wings partly open, then closed or trailed as the birds hit the surface head-first, sending up a plume of spray, to grip the prey a few metres under water and swallow it almost immediately. The shock of impact is taken by the specially adapted skull and the air sacs under the skin; the nostrils are also concealed in the unique bill. Gannets may dive obliquely from low heights, for example when taking offal behind a ship or in harbour: sometimes a dazzling sight as tens of the great birds join in. On the water they swim buoyantly with tails up; on land they waddle, seldom travelling far.

Nelson has shown that Gannets are extremely aggressive birds; their crowded colonies are a hubbub of loud *urrahs* and constant squabbles. Males display at their chosen sites, shaking their heads, leaning back with necks stretched and bills pointed downwards. This attracts a flying female, but she may be attacked first by her future mate. The display becomes mutual, with the noisy clashing of bills, and is used to reinforce the pair bond throughout the somewhat uneasy union.

A gannet colony may be on the ledges of a precipitous cliff or on comparatively gentle slopes; often other birds, especially guillemots, are nesting close by or are even tolerated among the lordly citizens. At a distance a pattern emerges, owing to the uniform spacing – just out of stabbing range – between each pair and their neighbours. The nests, built by both sexes, may be 60 cm. high, composed of land vegetation, seaweed, feathers, seaborne material, and earth from the vicinity, consolidated by droppings which give it stability on vertiginous sites. The single pale blue egg, laid from April onwards in the south, turns chalky white and then becomes stained brown. It is incubated by both parents in turn under their feet, as they have no brood patches, and hatches after about 44 days, held on top of the feet once it is 'pipped'. For about 2 weeks the adults brood the chick in its scanty greyish down and one remains on guard during the 90-day fledging period. The other forages, returning to feed the chick by regurgitation as it thrusts its head deep into the parental gape. There are several feeds a day and the young one becomes heavier than an adult by fledging time. Its first flight is gravity-assisted; if it cannot take off straight to sea, it must run the gauntlet of hostile adults to the cliff edge. Once water-borne it cannot take off again until it has lost weight and seems to be at the mercy of many enemies. But the continuing increase of the species shows that survival must be effective.

Immature birds apparently return to the area where they were reared when prospecting nest-sites in their turn. Non-breeders may even come to occupy nests, but in general they are to be found on the edges of the colony.

Some nesting places of the Gannet have a long history; there is archaeological evidence for the great St Kilda colony from the ninth century A.D.; both Ailsa Craig in the Firth of Clyde and the Bass Rock in the Forth were in existence early in the sixteenth century; Mykineskholm in the Faeroe Islands was active in the seventeenth century. A census can sometimes be made by ground counts but for large and inaccessible areas it is better to take photographs and count or calculate pairs from them. Operation Seafarer reported 16 colonies in Britain, Ireland and the Channel Isles in 1969–70, with an estimated population of 138,000 pairs. They ranged from (approximately) 52,000 pairs in the St Kilda group to 16 on Roareim in the Flannan Isles. Since Seafarer, breeding has begun on Fair Isle between Orkney and Shetland. The general increase follows a decline in the nineteenth century due mainly to human activity, especially at the American stations. Some young Gannets are still taken for food at Mykinesholm and from Sula Sgeir in the Hebrides.

*Adult Gannets in foreground with two immature birds
behind, first year bird (top) and second year bird
(below)*

Phalacrocorax carbo
CORMORANT
PHALACROCORACIDAE 90 cm. (body: 56 cm.)

Two races of this dark satanic bird breed in Northern Europe and are distinguishable for a short time in spring, when the southern *chinensis* shows much more frosty white on its head and neck than the typical *carbo*. The white thigh patches and brighter blue gloss on the head and under parts are other signs of the breeding plumage. The larger head, with a mane rather than a temporary crest, and more powerful hook-tipped bill help to tell adult Cormorants from Shags; their greater size only really counts when some comparison is possible. In the hand and sometimes at very close range the Cormorant's 14 tail feathers against the Shag's 12 can be counted. Juvenile and immature birds are more difficult: both species look generally darkish brown with paler throats and under parts in their first winter, but in their second and even third summers Cormorants show extensive white on the under parts and even breed in this plumage, whereas immature Shags are dark brown, though juveniles of the Mediterranean race, *P. aristotelis desmarestii*, have white under parts. The bare area of skin round the bill is lighter yellow on the Cormorant than on the Shag.

Unlike the restricted geographical status of the Gannet and the Shag, the Cormorant has a widespread Old World breeding distribution with outliers across the Atlantic. Over much of its Eurasian, East African and Australian ranges it is found inland, but in Northern Europe it is coastal or at least within reach of tidal waters. It breeds round Iceland, in the Faeroe Islands, along the coasts of western Scandinavia, Britain, Ireland and northern France, with colonies of the southern race in the Netherlands, Denmark and Germany. The autumn movement is a southward dispersal rather than a migration, though some birds may reach the Iberian Peninsula. Some English Cormorants winter as far inland as they can get, in Staffordshire.

Away from their colonies, Cormorants are most likely to be seen in 3 situations: in flight, with neck stretched and feet under the tail; on the water, swimming low down and ready to submerge; and on perches from sand banks to buoys, buildings and trees, when the wings are often spread heraldically. This is generally supposed to be a drying posture because the Cormorant's waterproofing is not very efficient; it has also been suggested that it aids digestion. Cormorants usually fly with powerful beats of their rather broad wings, but also glide and even soar on high, when they could be confused with storks and cranes. Sometimes parties fly in line or V-formation, for example up rivers to inland feeding places: their silhouette prevents confusion with ducks, geese or divers, as it does on the water where the bill is inclined upward.

Fishing Cormorants may prospect with heads below the surface; when they dive, the whole body leaves the water in an arc or, less often, is quietly submerged. Propulsion under water is by the webbed feet working together. Dives are seldom deeper than 10 m. or longer than a minute, usually about half that time, and prey is swallowed on the surface, often after some juggling in the bill. Fish taken at sea are mostly those also sought by man and include many flatfish; in fresh water depredations on trout may be balanced by relieving their pressure on young salmon (D. H. Mills).

The vocabulary of the Cormorant is mainly

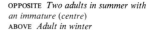

OPPOSITE *Two adults in summer with an immature (centre)*
ABOVE *Adult in winter*

exercised at the breeding colony where a great variety of hoarse croaking calls and other notes have been described, associated with the advertising and mutual displays, which include twisting the neck and exposing the yellow gape with neck stretched. The female may take the more active part in these, though the male initiates advances by presenting her with sticks (A. F. J. Portelje).

Many of the Cormorant's breeding stations are reasonably accessible, on the flat or sloping tops of stacks and headlands; sometimes they are on low islands and, in the Netherlands and

generally throughout the inland range, they are in trees, often shared with herons and other large waterbirds. Grey Herons, *Ardea cinerea*, can apparently switch their sites from reedbeds to trees in spite of the extra architectural skill needed; evidently Cormorants can also build a solid nest of sticks aloft as well as a heap of sea-weed, straws and debris on a cliff. The male supplies most of the material and the female places it. The whole eventually becomes plastered with droppings. The rather elongated, pale blue eggs with their chalky covering, soon to be stained, are laid, from early April in the south, at about

2-day intervals: 3 or 5 is the usual clutch. Incu-bation may start during laying and is shared by both parents for about 4 weeks. The chicks when hatched are naked, blind and blackish. Their eyes open after about 5 days as the dark brown down grows. They are fed by their parents with regurgitated fish and even watered in hot wea-ther. After some 5 weeks they begin to scramble about, but do not fly for 7 or 8 weeks and become fully independent several weeks later, when par-ties sit like brown bottles on the rocks.

For Operation Seafarer results, see under the Shag.

Phalacrocorax aristotelis
SHAG
PHALACROCORACIDAE 76 cm. (body: 46 cm.)

The generic name means 'bald crow' (or raven), a somewhat inappropriate description of this species in its full spring plumage when for a few weeks it sports a tufted crest worthy of the immortal Tintin. Apart from this temporary adornment and its generally bottle-green gloss, the Shag's main differences from the Cormorant in all plumages have been described under that species. The thin bill of the juvenile as compared to the adult is worth noting. Full plumage is normally assumed when the birds are 2 years old though some may breed at that age when still partly immature in appearance.

The Shag's breeding distribution in Northern Europe is almost identical with the Cormorant's coastal range. It is absent from the low-lying shores of Holland, Denmark and Germany, but extends into the Mediterranean as far as the Black Sea and Cyprus. Like the Cormorant it disperses in autumn rather than migrates; birds from Britain cross the North Sea and the English Channel and one at least has reached Spain. The Icelandic and north Scandinavian populations must also move south.

Altogether more maritime than the Cormorant, the Shag is much less inclined to perch, except when it has been driven inland by a storm. Some years ago a party in these straits used to resort to a gasometer by the River Thames at Reading. Shags are usually seen sitting in force on low skerries, to be washed off by the tide, when they swim low in the water like so many animated periscopes. Rafts of many hundreds may occur in some areas, for example the sheltered waters of the Isles of Scilly (John Parslow). They normally dive with a curved leap like a Cormorant; slow submersion is less usual. Their dives appear to be longer than their relative's, averaging between 45 seconds and a minute. The food taken has been the subject of several studies with somewhat different results. About a third of the fish taken in Loch Ewe in the Scottish West Highlands were of 'economic value'; half of them were herrings. But earlier results in Cornwall suggested that sand-eels were the main prey, which was to some extent supported by an examination of birds from the Firth of Clyde. No doubt the composition of the diet varies locally and seasonally; crustaceans are taken and, presumably, molluscs since many Shags from the Farne Islands off the north-east English coast died in 1968 as a result of 'paralytic shellfish poisoning'.

The main described display is the female's solicitation of the male on or near the nest. She throws her neck back, turns her head towards the male and moves it from side to side, quivering the loose skin round her throat. Then she darts her head at him, exposing the bright yellow gape, cocking her tail and uttering hissing and clicking noises. The male stretches head and bill in the air and gapes; his call is a series of croaks, uttered near or at the nest. Sitting birds also gape and hiss at intruders but, compared to most European sea birds, Shags are remarkably silent.

The general coastal breeding distribution of the Cormorant may coincide with the Shag's, but there are many stretches where one is present and not the other. Shag colonies are more dispersed and the nest-sites often more inaccessible, on steep cliffs among Razorbills and Kittiwakes – as on the Farne Islands – or on the walls of sea caves. Elsewhere they nest under boulders on talus slopes with gulls as neighbours. They are not known to breed on fresh water. The nest is built mainly of seaweeds, but may include heather stems, sticks and debris, with a finer lining. During the season it becomes caked with droppings and the remains of meals. In Britain and Ireland laying generally begins in April, but odd pairs may start as early as the end of January; the clutch is usually of 3 pale blue eggs, covered by a patchy chalky deposit and becoming stained during incubation, which usually starts with the second egg and lasts 30 days, both parents participating. The naked brown-skinned chicks are brooded for about 2 weeks while their pale brown down grows, and are fed by regurgitation. They leave the nest after 7 or 8 weeks but continue to be fed for at least another 4 weeks. Although nests with eggs may be found in August, there appears to be no proof of genuine second broods. As well as their breeding cliffs, Shags have favourite sites where they may be found year after year without ever nesting at them.

Cormorants and Shags are among the easier sea birds for census work and can often be counted directly at their colonies, though Shags nesting under boulders or in caves are more difficult. The Operation Seafarer figure for Cormorants in 1969–70 was just over 8100 pairs, of which about 40 per cent were in Scotland. The Shag was nearly 4 times more numerous with about 31,600 pairs, of which 25,000 were in Scotland. In spite of some local fluctuations, the Shag has generally increased in recent years, probably due to greater protection; the evidence for the Cormorant, though it has increased in some parts, is less conclusive over the whole British area.

An adult in summer plumage (left), in winter plumage
(centre) and an immature bird (right)

Aythya marila
SCAUP
ANATIDAE 48 cm. (body: 32 cm.)

Although some surface-feeding ducks are associated with salt water, none has been included, because they are not primarily marine at any season. The Scaup (lower pair on plate) certainly prefers sheltered coasts and estuaries but for much of the year it is a sea duck. The male can be confused with other dark-headed drakes at a distance but is distinctive under reasonable conditions: black at both ends and grey in the middle. Although female Tufted Ducks, *A. fuligula*, often show some white round the bill, the adult female Scaup shows much more, with a clearly defined margin. Difficulties arise between immatures of both sexes and female and immature Tufted Ducks, all showing a partial white area. During October most young male Scaups begin to show some vermiculation on the back, and Tufted males become blacker. At close range the Scaup's more rounded body – though no *Aythya* ducks show much tail in the water – larger head, with no hint of crest, and broader bill are additional points. The male retains the vermiculated back in eclipse (August–November); both sexes show a white wing-bar in flight.

The Scaup breeds round the world, roughly between 60° and 70°N, with a big gap in eastern North America. Its European range is from Iceland, where it is common, and the Faeroe Islands through northern Scandinavia to western Russia, with outliers in the Baltic and sporadic nesting in Scotland. The wintering areas are from the western Baltic to Ireland and the French Channel coast; and in the Mediterranean, Black and Caspian seas. M. A. Ogilvie believes that the Iceland population keeps separate; he gives a total north-west European winter figure of 150,000 birds, half of them in the Baltic. But the concentration in the Firth of Forth, said to be due to grain from Edinburgh's sewage outfalls, was once estimated at 40,000; in December 1972 it was about 25,000 out of a total British and Irish estuarine population of 26,555 birds.

This is a flocking species, favouring rather loosely clotted aggregations both in flight and when feeding; only odd birds occur inland. Scaup typically dive for their food, mainly young mussels and other shellfish with some crustaceans; dives average 30 seconds and are up to 6 m. deep. Large prey is swallowed on the surface. In summer insects and the buds and seeds of aquatic plants are eaten.

Normally silent, the male Scaup utters a crooning *wa-hoo* when courting and the female incites him with a low *arrr*. His displays include head-throwing backwards and exposing the speculum by 'preening' actions, to which the female may respond in kind. Scaup breed on the islands or shores of tundra and moorland waters, often in colonies of gulls and terns. The rather exposed nest is lined with sooty-coloured down and contains from 7 to 11 elongated greenish-grey eggs. The downy young hatch after 3½

to 4 weeks incubation by the female, who also normally tends them alone until they fly at 5 to 6 weeks.

Bucephala clangula
GOLDENEYE
ANATIDAE Male 46 cm. (body: 30 cm.); female smaller.

Some birds have a single feature which is a key to their identification: such is the Goldeneye's 'triangular' head, an effect due to the small bill and domed crown. A male in full fig, attained in his second winter, can only really be confused with Barrow's Goldeneye. Their females are even more alike, with head shape the best clue. Males in eclipse (August to late autumn) resemble females but have darker heads; young males are also similar, but have dark bills and no clear neck ring. There is a broad white wing-bar in all plumages.

Goldeneye breed throughout the conifer taiga zone of the northern hemisphere, with some southerly outliers, including Scotland since 1970, but not Iceland, the province of Barrow's Goldeneye. In winter birds are found in the British area, the western Baltic and southward across Europe to the Mediterranean, Black and Caspian seas. There may be 170,000 pairs nesting in Finland and western Russia, and a winter population in north-western Europe of 150,000 birds, two-thirds in the Baltic, where some thousands also moult in late summer.

Short-necked in silhouette, the Goldeneye flies with a singing sound, most pronounced from adult males. These may be in a distinct minority in southern wintering areas and the sex ratio may vary locally. Seldom seen on land, Goldeneye in winter feed close to the shore in small parties, often diving in concert for about half a minute. They search the bottom with their short, serrated bills, taking mainly small crustaceans (especially in salt water) and molluscs; in summer on fresh water insect larvae and other aquatic animals are eaten. Silent except in display, the male has a rattling call and the female a gruff croak.

The male Goldeneye is renowned for the number and complexity of his displays. P. A. Johnsgard regards 'bowsprit-pumping' as the most frequent: the neck is repeatedly extended upward and retracted in silence; the female may respond with similar movements. Even more striking is the male's 'head-throw' backwards with accompanying spurt of water from the feet; this may be seen in winter.

The female perches when searching for her tree-hole nest-site (nestboxes are used freely); once tenanted, it is entered non-stop from flight. The 8 to 11 bluish-green eggs are laid on very pale grey down, from mid-April in the south, and incubated for about 4 weeks by the female, with the male nearby. But she alone tends the brown and white ducklings after they drop from the nest, sometimes leading them over 3 km. to a pool or lake. Fledging takes 7 to 8 weeks.

Scaups in foreground, female (above), male (below).
In background, a female Goldeneye (above)
and a male (below)

Barrow's Goldeneye, *B. islandica*, is a primarily west North American duck which breeds
in Iceland and is a rare vagrant elsewhere in
Europe. The male has a white crescent on the
cheek of his rounded, purple-glossed head (green
on Goldeneye), and large spots rather than bars
on the closed wing; the female's bill is all yellow
in spring. In treeless Iceland the nest is in a rock
crevice. Another related North American duck,
the little Bufflehead, *B. albeola*, has also wan-
dered occasionally to European waters.

Clangula hyemalis
LONG-TAILED DUCK

ANATIDAE 43 cm. (body: 30 cm.); Drake's tail feathers may add another 13 cm.

This small sea duck, whose tubby form allows it to be mistaken for a grebe at distances where the snub-nosed bill cannot be seen, is one of the world's most northerly breeding species, reaching 82°N on Ellesmere Island. It is credited with dives of nearly 60 m. and has survived an enormous mortality as a result of man's activities, from fishing nets in the Great Lakes to contamination by oil in the Baltic.

The various plumages are essentially combinations of white and shades of brown, white predominating in winter, brown in summer; the small head with its rather abrupt forehead and the stubby bill are distinctive at all ages. Only the adult drake has the long tail, which appears thinner and whippier than that of the Pintail, *Anas acuta*, the only other long-tailed duck in Northern Europe. The winter plumage of both sexes is shown opposite, the summer dress on this page. This is acquired by the drake between February and June: except for the cheeks, the head, neck, and breast become dark brown; shoulders and back are brighter, with black-centred feathers. Losing his tail feathers, he goes into eclipse in late summer and into winter dress after October. The summer duck has a dark brown head and upper parts and a light brown breast. The fluffy brown and white ducklings turn into rather dull editions of the duck, with greyish bills and legs; by the end of the year young drakes show white shoulder patches.

The distribution of the Long-tailed Duck (Oldsquaw in North America) spans the northern hemisphere; it breeds all along the northern coasts of Eurasia and North America, extending into many of the archipelagos and islands of the Arctic Ocean, including Greenland and Iceland. The wintering area is mainly not far south of the breeding range, in the Atlantic and Pacific oceans and on the Great Lakes, though elsewhere Long-tailed Ducks are uncommon inland, usually to be noted only in ones and twos. But tens of thousand fly over Finland on spring migration 'cutting their corners' if visibility is bad on the coast (G. Bergman).

Normally social, Long-tailed Ducks form noisy parties, which apparently delight in rough seas. When they take wing, they usually fly low over the waves with a swinging action that shows the birds now white, now dark, like a flock of waders; the wing beat is peculiar, not rising high above the body on the upstroke, but lower than other ducks' on the downstroke, the wing-tips appearing to move backwards (Ludlow Griscom).

The call of the drake is one of those natural sounds on the verbalization of which no 2 observers agree. According to *The Handbook of British Birds*, it is 'a loud resonant polysyllabic note, variously rendered "ow-ow-owdl-ow", "cah-cah-coralwee", "caloo-caloo", etc.' But it is acknowledged to be musically attractive and has been compared to distant bagpipes, presumably in its Scottish winter quarters, and to baying hounds. The call is much used in communal display when several drakes surround a duck, tails aloft, necks stretched and then lowered towards the duck, with the bow typical of many anatid displays, and the call. Another action characteristic of the family is to throw the head back, calling as it comes forward again. Drakes also chase each other and both sexes may stretch their necks along the surface.

Long-tailed Ducks feed mainly on marine animals, a great variety of molluscs, crustaceans and other bottom-living forms such as annelid

OPPOSITE *Adults in winter, female (above), male (below)*
BELOW *Male in summer*

worms, for which they make their deep dives; in summer they take many insects at all stages from the tundra pools; and small fish are also on their menu.

Breeding takes place from late May right into July according to latitude. Islands in freshwater lakes and fjords are a favourite habitat, where the birds nest under the protection of terns and gulls. The open tundra and the alpine zones in Scandinavia also provide sites for the simple nest of local materials and very dark, light-centred down, under cover of heather, dwarf willows, or stones. The usual clutch is 6 to 8

smooth, rather pointed olive-buff to yellowish eggs which the duck incubates for about $3\frac{1}{2}$ weeks, guarded at first by the drake, who then joins a 'club' of his fellows. The young are fed initially by the duck – sometimes broods combine – and fledge in about 5 weeks.

Its very large numbers, before man's threat to its environment became so marked, have to some extent buffered the Long-tailed Duck against disaster; for how long no one knows. But every effort should be made to conserve the breeding places of this delightful and totally harmless little duck.

Melanitta fusca
VELVET SCOTER

ANATIDAE 56 cm. (body: 36 cm.)

The scoters are a group of 3 largish sea ducks with dark plumages and pointed tails, distinguished from each other by their head and bill patterns, and in general for their vulnerability to oil pollution. This species is known as the White-winged Scoter in America, descriptive of the character that separates it at a distance from the other 2, though it is only the speculum on the secondaries which is white. Close-up, the male shows a small white patch under the whitish eye, a parti-coloured bill with a small black basal knob and red feet with blackish webs. In eclipse (July onwards) he merely becomes duller, and browner underneath. The dark brown female, with faintly barred under parts, and the immatures of both sexes are much alike, with 2 white facial spots which become fainter with age; one may disappear altogether. The female's feet are darker than the male's; those of young males are reddish yellow with dark webs, while young females have orange-pink feet with blackish webs; all have dark brown eyes. Males acquire full plumage by their second winter.

The Velvet Scoter is another duck with a discontinuous breeding range round the northern hemisphere, mainly between 50° and 70°N in the taiga and forest tundra zones, stretching many miles inland. There are 3 distinct areas and the east Asian and American populations have been regarded as a separate species, *M. deglandi*. The European breeding range is in the upper Baltic and through western and northern Scandinavia into western Russia, expanding in latitude eastwards. The breeding populations move down to the coast after nesting. Some remain beyond the arctic circle in Norway; other areas are the western Baltic, the North Sea and along the French coast to northern Iberia. Discrete groups winter in the south-west Black Sea and Sea of Marmara, and in the south-east of the Caspian Sea. E. Merikallio estimated the Finnish breeding population at 5000 to 8000 pairs in 1958. Nearly 30,000 winter in the Baltic, and under 1000 round Britain (M. A. Ogilvie), but as many as 45,000, of which 80 per cent are adult males, moult in late summer in Danish waters (A. H. Joensen).

Scoters are traditionally depicted at home on the rolling deep, with this species the hardiest of all, usually to be seen in quite small parties; occasionally it may flock with the Common Scoter. Velvet Scoters take off with difficulty, flying low but sometimes well clear of the water. They may rest on the shore but are poor walkers. When diving, their wings may be partly open and kept so under water, possibly helping navigation; the birds usually stay down less than a minute but may reach depths variously estimated as 12 to 20 m. and are at risk in some areas from fishermen's nets. Their main prey is molluscs, especially mussels, to tackle which the powerful bills of the group are obviously well adapted; crustaceans, mainly small crabs, are also taken,

and in summer there is a change to fresh water animals, worms and parts of aquatic plants.

Like the Surf Scoter, the Velvet Scoter appears to be silent except in display, when the male whistles and rattles and the female has a hoarse croak much as attributed to several sea ducks. M. T. Myres has described a chin-lifting display by the female, accompanied by a 'very thin whistle' and clearly, according to P. A. Johnsgard, a form of enticement to the male. Both sexes have a ritualized drinking action. Males attack each other under water or swim rapidly on the surface with necks stretched forward in threat. Before mating, the male may flick the water with his bill, usually following this by ritual preening movements. Mating takes place on the water, the female inviting it by lying on the surface.

The breeding habitat ranges from woodland round lakes and wooded islands in the Baltic to bare mountainous areas and tundra in the north. There is a tendency to nest in colonies of gulls and terns, probably resulting in some protection from other enemies, though J. Koskimies has reported attacks on young scoters by large gulls in his Finnish study area. The nest scrape is usually well hidden in vegetation and lined with neighbouring plant material and thick dark brown down. The clutch is typically of 7 to 9 smooth, creamy buff eggs laid late in May in the Baltic and in June further north. They hatch after about 4 weeks, incubated solely by the female, who is deserted by the male. The ducklings have down in shades of brown with a white throat and cheeks. Their mother tends to leave them for long periods during fledging and, in the densely populated islands of the Gulf of Bothnia, 'broods' of up to 100 young may form, tended by a single female (O. Hildén). They become independent at 4 to 5 weeks, flying when about 6 or 7 weeks old. They are at least 2 years old before they begin to breed in their turn.

Melanitta perspicillata
SURF SCOTER

ANATIDAE 53 cm. (body: 37 cm.)

The male of this North American species is distinguished by 2 white areas, on crown and nape, and by the heavy supra-Bardolphian bill, brightly coloured red, white and yellow. Apart from the red feet, the rest of the plumage is black, partly glossed green or purple. Females and immature birds are very hard to tell from similar plumages of the Velvet Scoter; they have no wing-bar but this difference may not show when they are on a rough sea. Some adult females, however, have a white patch on the nape like the males.

There have been some hundreds of records of Surf Scoters along the north-western coasts of Europe, so this is a rarity to be looked out for, especially in the winter half of the year when birds wander from the nearest breeding areas in Newfoundland and eastern Canada. Their habits at sea resemble those of their 2 relatives.

Adult Velvet Scoters male (below), female (above)

Melanitta nigra
COMMON SCOTER
ANATIDAE 48 cm. (body: 32 cm.)

The smallest scoter has the darkest male plumage, relieved only by the apricot yellow on the otherwise black bill with its basal knob. The gloss is somewhat dulled in the eclipse plumage (July onwards) and the under parts become browner, but not noticeably in the field. Surprisingly noticeable, however, are the female's pale cheeks, a feature shared with the Red-crested Pochard, *Netta rufina*, a species unlikely often to be in juxtaposition. Young birds of both sexes are very like adult females but lighter both above and below; the males begin to show some black in their first autumn but transition is not complete until the following autumn.

This species has a more restricted range than the Velvet Scoter. The race *americana* breeds in east Siberia, western Alaska and a few Canadian localities; the typical *nigra* in Iceland, Svalbard (rare), the Faeroe Islands, Ireland and Scotland, more commonly in western and northern Scandinavia east to Russia, in forest, tundra, moorland and on some low-lying lochs in Scotland and Ireland. The winter movement coastward and southward is much as performed by the Velvet Scoter but extends to North Africa and does not include the Black and Caspian seas. The sex ratio may vary markedly in different areas. The wintering figure for north-western Europe is about 130,000 mostly in the Baltic area, but larger numbers have been estimated there during the moult migration in late summer (A. H. Joensen). There may be about 20,000 birds in the British area, where non-breeders may be seen throughout the summer, and there is a marked passage in spring through the Straits of Dover.

Common Scoters at ease swim buoyantly, holding their pointed tails up, but sink like Shags if suspicious. After head-shaking 'intention movements', they take off more smoothly than Velvet Scoters and may fly in great ragged columns over the sea, or over the land, as in Denmark when crossing from the Baltic to their western moulting ground or over Finland in their spring migration northward (G. Bergman). Wing-beats are rapid and a whistling sound is generated by the narrow outer primaries of the males. They may haul out on sandbanks to rest, but move awkwardly on land. It is another matter in the water when they dive after mussels and other shellfish, crustaceans and, in summer, small freshwater animals, also taking some plant buds and tubers. The wings are sometimes opened for the dive, which usually lasts half a minute and may go down 9 m.

This is the most vocal of the scoters because of the male's piping call heard from flocks at sea from late winter into spring, with an additional rattling note in autumn. The female utters a grating whistle in reply to the male as she 'preens' ritually. He may respond by 'snapping' his tail, then rushing across the water beside her. But P. A. Johnsgard observes that many of the male's

displays are only slightly modified forms of 'ordinary comfort movements'. Before mating, he may stand up in the water, and may repeat some of his displays after mounting.

The nest is usually near water, often on an island. Several females may build close together, lining their scrapes with grass stems and dark brown, light-centred down. The typical clutch of 6 to 9 pale creamy to buff eggs is laid from late May in the south and hatches in 27 to 31 days, incubated by the female alone, the male soon absenting himself altogether. The ducklings in down are dark brown above, whitish beneath from cheeks to belly. Tended by the female, they fledge in 6 to 7 weeks.

OPPOSITE *Adult female (above), male (below)*
BELOW *Harlequin male*

Histrionicus histrionicus
HARLEQUIN DUCK
ANATIDAE 44 cm. (body: 29 cm.)

Another Iceland speciality, shown here in black and white, which reveals the remarkable patterning of black-bordered white streaks on a dark background of blue grey. There is a touch of chestnut on the side of the crown and an extended patch on the flanks. The female is mainly dark brown, mottled with white below and with white marks on head and wing, leading to possible confusion with the female Long-tailed Duck. Both sexes have a glossy purple speculum, rather pointed tail, a stubby bluish bill with

white nail and bluish legs with black webs. The male in eclipse (July onwards) loses much of his finery but remains slaty grey and distinct from the female. Juveniles resemble her and do not attain full plumage until their second year.

The breeding range is primarily east Asian and North American, but the resident Iceland population has recently been estimated by F. Guðmundsson at about 5000 pairs. Wanderers appear on the coasts of north-west Europe. Not only favouring the fastest rivers when breeding, Harlequins are fond of rough seas, feeding off the rocks by diving, sometimes from the wing,

after molluscs and crustaceans, taking insect larvae in summer. Parties swim close together, sometimes in apparently precise formations, and this is an agile duck on land. In spite of his striking plumage the male does not seem to have elaborate displays, nodding his head and flapping his wings. He has a staccato call and the female a hoarse croak. Harlequins nest colonially on scrub-clad river islets, laying, from the end of May, 6 to 8 pale creamy eggs in a lining of light brown down. Incubated by the female, they hatch after 27 to 32 days and the young fly in under 7 weeks.

Somateria mollissima
EIDER

ANATIDAE 58 cm. (body: 38 cm.)

The largest and most numerous European sea duck is also the best known, having given its name to a comforting article of bedding and boasting a recorded history back to seventh century St Cuthbert. The adult male is unmistakable, but takes up to 4 years to reach full plumage, some white areas appearing in the first summer. The young male shares with the adult in eclipse (July onwards) a curving light brown band from the bill over the eye. The adult retains his white forewing, being otherwise generally blackish brown. Juveniles resemble the brown, black-barred female, who has a definite brownish speculum between 2 narrow paler bars.

The Eider's breeding range is divided between the North Atlantic and the North Pacific. The North European distribution covers Iceland, with probably half a million pairs; the arctic archipelagos; the Faeroe Islands, which have a resident race *faeroeensis*, rather smaller than the typical *mollissima* and with darker female plumage; Scandinavia and the Baltic, which hold perhaps 300,000 pairs; the Netherlands; Britain with about 10,000 pairs and spreading; Ireland (local in north), and Brittany, recently colonized. This huge population is resident in ice-free regions, but the arctic multitudes come south in autumn, are beginning to winter inland in Germany and Switzerland and are found as far south as the delta of the Rhône.

Almost entirely marine, Eiders are seen at all times in black and white rafts off coasts both rocky and low-lying. In spring the cooing chorus of the males as they pursue their apparently ceaseless bickerings and courtship is most evocative. The birds haul out to rest and preen, especially in spring and autumn, waddling competently on land; but they usually roost at sea. They take off heavily from water and fly low over it in wavy lines. Their dives are mainly in shallow water, seldom for more than 45 seconds and they bring up a great variety of shellfish, with mussels predominating, crustaceans, echinoderms and coelenterates. Some insects, offal and seaweed are also taken. Sometimes the diving parties are joined by gulls, which rob the Eiders when they surface.

The male Eider has a number of displays, including actions of the head associated with the cooing call and ritualized comfort movements derived from bathing, flapping the wings and stretching upward. The female invites the male to mate by lifting her chin, then gradually lies prone on the water, while he goes through some of his repertoire before mounting. She has single and double-note calls in response to displays, and makes the hoarse sound common to diving ducks.

Although occasionally found breeding inland, the vast majority of Eiders nest on the coast or on offshore islands. They are highly colonial; this habit has been exploited in Iceland to build up large Eider farms, to which the birds are attracted by prepared stone 'nests'. The scrape is lined with the famous light grey, pale-centred down and the clutch, usually of 4 to 6 large, greenish eggs, is laid from late April in the south. The male often remains near his incubating mate but takes no part in raising the family. She is reluctant to leave the nest during the 4 week incubation, and defecates over the eggs if disturbed. On Eider farms and protected colonies like the Farne Islands, females may be handled on their nests. The blackish ducklings are taken at once to the sea, where 'aunts' (?failed breeders) may appear to join the female in looking after them and broods frequently combine. The young fledge in 8½ to 10½ weeks; they are much at risk to large gulls in some areas.

Somateria spectabilis
KING EIDER

ANATIDAE 56 cm. (body: 36 cm.)

Males in full plumage are absolutely distinctive but take several years to attain it. The female is a brighter brown than the common Eider, with an unstreaked throat and more pronounced black spots on the upper parts. Juveniles in general resemble the female. This is a high arctic species with circumpolar distribution and ranks as European by nesting in north-western Russia, Novaya Zemlya, Svalbard, occasionally in Iceland, usually a mixed mating. Birds occur regularly in winter on Norwegian, less often on British coasts. The King Eider resembles its relative in many respects, but nests inland and is said to dive deeper and for longer.

Another arctic duck from further east, the Spectacled Eider, *S. fischeri*, is a rare winter visitor to extreme Northern Europe; both sexes have a large pale patch round the eye and the adult male's head is green.

Polysticta stelleri
STELLER'S EIDER

ANATIDAE 46 cm. (body: 30 cm.)

This beautiful pointed-tailed sea duck may be colonizing Norway as it is now present all the year in Varanger Fjord in some numbers. It breeds from time to time in arctic Russia. The male is mainly black and white above, with green patches on the white head, and chestnut-buff below. The female is very dark brown, with a purple speculum; juveniles are much lighter.

*In foreground, adult Eiders, male (right) and female
(left); in midground, immature male Eider (above)
with adult male King Eider (below); in background
mixed group*

Mergus serrator
RED-BREASTED MERGANSER
ANATIDAE 58 cm. (body: 36 cm.)

The scientific specific name refers to one salient character of this group of diving ducks: their 'saw bill', an adaptation for gripping slippery fish, for example the butterfish or spotted gunnel, *Centronotus gunnellus*. The accompanying thinness of the mandibles seems unducklike and leads to confusion in the field with cormorants, divers and especially grebes. But the wayward crest on both sexes of this merganser is quite unlike that of the Great Crested Grebe, the nearest in size. The male also looks rather like a rakish Mallard, *Anas platyrhynchos*, but here the different bill helps. Confusion with the male Goosander is less likely; in flight this species shows less white on the wing, the broad white speculum being bounded by 2 black bars, whereas the black on the Goosander is indistinct and patchy. The moult to eclipse plumage begins in spring and goes on until September, full plumage being assumed again only 2 months later. This means that odd-looking males are about with their mates for several months and come to look very like them, except for their white forewings. Juveniles resemble females but have greyer backs and short crests; they acquire full plumage in their second winter. The female may be told from the maned Goosander by her crest and by the undefined frontier between chestnut-brown head and the dull white throat. Also the back is brownish rather than clear grey. The speculum agrees with the male's, but the forewing is greyish.

This is another duck with a rather discontinuous and irregular breeding distribution round the northern hemisphere, mainly between 60° and 70°N, with some curious outliers. The North European range is from Iceland to the Faeroe Islands, north-western Britain, where there has been a recent spread south, Ireland, Scandinavia, with perhaps 10,000 pairs in Finland (E. Merikallio), and the Baltic coasts to western Russia, favouring in general 'clear waters abounding in fish' (K. H. Voous). Mergansers are resident in the western ice-free part of their range but other populations migrate south, occupying the North Sea and Channel coasts on to Biscay, round Iberia and into the northern Mediterranean and the Black Sea. A. H. Joensen suggests that about 20,000 birds, of which at least 12,000 are males, moult in Danish waters; peak numbers are present in mid-July. The males are found in shallow water in the early morning but have daytime roosts about 4 km. offshore; females do not concentrate when moulting. M. A. Ogilvie suggests a winter population for north-western Europe of about 40,000 birds, largely estuarine, of which up to a quarter may be round Britain and Ireland. Females and younger birds may migrate further than males.

Red-breasted Mergansers may be seen in pairs, small parties, occasionally larger flocks, on both salt and fresh water. They fly readily, making a whistling sound, and may flight from their feeding grounds to roost on the open sea. They can walk quite well in spite of the position of the legs far back on the body, but are not much seen on land. They generally swim low in the water and often progress with head under water when fishing. Dives, by leaping or quiet submersion, are usually up to half a minute long and in water 2 to 4 m. deep. A variety of small fish is caught in sea, lake or river, making up probably three-quarters of the diet. Off the Finnish archipelago in the eastern Baltic sticklebacks are the main prey in spring (P. Bagge *et al.*). Generally, crustaceans, worms, small molluscs and insects are also taken. Mass-feeding in winter is recorded for this species as for the Goosander.

The female Merganser is not very active in display but remains, according to P. A. Johnsgard, aggressive to the male and has a harsh *krrr* call. The male has a closed-wing 'sprint' over the surface and 'an extremely complex and variable sequence' of unique actions called the *Knicks*, after the German for a curtsey. The main features are a stretching up of the neck from a tense crouched position to the 'salute', uttering a catlike *yeow*, changing to the extraordinary 'curtsey' with neck on the water, bill wide open for another *yeow*, the hind quarters raised and the tail dipped. The bird finishes with neck bent, crest raised and tail bent downward. Some of these actions can take place on land, and are motivated either as threat or courtship. The *Knicks* may be performed again just before mating, together with various ritualized comfort movements. After mounting, the male may repeat the *Knicks*, then bathe or 'sprint', finally plunging under the surface (R. G. Adams).

Breeding both by fresh and salt water, the female Merganser usually conceals her nest well in thick vegetation with a tunnel approach, under rocks, even in a wide burrow. It is lined with plant stems and dark grey-brown down with pale centres. The clutch is usually of 7 to 12 creamy to pale greenish eggs and may be laid from mid-May in the south of the range. The eggs, incubated by the female, hatch in 4 to 5 weeks and may be left for periods safe and warm in the down. The ducklings are particularly attractive, dark above and white below, with chestnut cheeks and a chestnut spot by the eye. The female alone looks after them, but frequently several combine their broods and flocks of juveniles may occur. The fledging period is about 8½ weeks.

Male (left), female (centre) and male in eclipse (right)

Mergus merganser
GOOSANDER
ANATIDAE Male 66 cm. (body: 46 cm.);
female smaller.

The specific and common names of the largest
'saw-bill' reflect early doubts as to its proven-
ance: was it a goose or a duck? The modern view
relates the saw-bills, in spite of superficial differences, to the goldeneye *Bucephala*. The male
is certainly one of the most impressive waterfowl, especially if seen in the brief glory of his
salmon-pink under parts. But, as with the Red-
breasted Merganser, eclipse begins in spring and
lasts until autumn: in it the male resembles the
female but with white forewing and dark, brownish back. The female has a much 'cleaner' plumage than the Merganser, with a defined white
collar. Juveniles resemble her but young males
begin to show some adult plumage in their first
winter. Immature birds are hard to tell from
Red-breasted Mergansers, though at all times
the rounded head is a distinction.

The breeding distribution is of the same general pattern as the Red-breasted Merganser
(across the Atlantic the Goosander is called the
Common or American Merganser), but further
south, largely between 50° and 60°N and with
several outlying enclaves. In Northern Europe
the range runs from Iceland, excluding the
Faeroe Islands, to northern Britain (fairly recent
expansion from Scotland into England), Scandinavia and the Baltic coasts to a broad band
through western Russian, and principally near
wooded inland waters but also on sheltered
marine inlets. There are enclaves in West Germany and Switzerland. The population in the
ice-free west is resident, even in Iceland, but
there is a considerable migration to the Channel
coasts and south-east over Europe to the Black
Sea. Finland, with 4000 pairs (E. Merikallio),
has a fairly high breeding population; the winter
strength in north-west Europe is about 70,000
birds, with 2500 to 5000 mainly on fresh water
in Britain, where it is less numerous than the
Merganser; it is absent from Ireland. Sex ratios
in winter vary; adult males may be less migratory than females and immature 'brownheads'.

At a distance, swimming high in the water, a
party of Goosander males looks very black and
white and might be confused with the much
smaller Goldeneye. But very often they swim
low, especially if ill at ease. Head movements
run through the group as an intention to take-
off, which they do with some difficulty, usually
flying low with rapid beats and a whistling
sound. On migration they are believed to travel
at a height. In spite of its size and cigar-shaped
body the Goosander is relatively agile on land,
walking partly upright and even able to run. It
feeds mostly by day, often 'exploring' with head
down, then diving with a leap or sinking silently,
to travel a considerable distance submerged in
about half a minute, descending from 2 to 4 m.,

probably the range of depth at its feeding
grounds. A very high proportion of the diet is
fish, of many species from fresh and salt water
and up to 30 cm. in length; 50 small fish have
been taken from a single stomach. Crustaceans,
insects, frogs and worms are also eaten. M. A.
Ogilvie remarks that the modern coexistence of
Goosanders and Mergansers in the same habitats is an interesting ecological situation, perhaps based on the different size of prey taken.

Goosanders are noted for their communal
feeding, similar to that of many passerine birds
on land. As the leaders dive, those behind fly
over them to get in front, all apparently in a
great state of excitement. Gulls may join the
flock and attempt to parasitize the Goosanders,
as they do Eiders. Mass feeding is particularly
noticeable on some Swedish lakes and on the
Dutch IJsselmeer, where a single flock may number 10,000 birds. Goosanders also joined in the
mass feeding by a flock of Smews in the same
area (L. Nilsson).

The female Goosander is even less coopera-
tive in display than the Red-breasted Merganser,
attacking her suitors with jabs of the bill and
warning them off with the harsh *karrr* call shared
by so many diving ducks (P. A. Johnsgard). The
call, however, is also used to incite the male;
after a spurning thrust at one bird, the female
spurts forward, calling, and preceded by a more
favoured male who shows her the back of his
head in bulbous outline. Males also attack each
other both on and under the surface. The commonest display is an extension of the neck, with
raising of the crown feathers and a repeated
guitar-like call: *uig-a*. The most elaborate action
described by Johnsgard is a form of 'salute' (see
Red-breasted Merganser) in which the neck is
stretched and bill held briefly vertically upward,
with 'a faint, high-pitched, bell-like note' before
relaxation. There are also several ritualized comfort movements, and mutual 'drinking' which
features largely in the routine leading up to
mating on the water. After it, the male swims
away, showing the back of his head and giving
the *uig-a* call, while his mate bathes.

The traditional breeding habitat is coniferous
taiga or other woodland studded with lakes and
traversed by rivers. Here the female chooses a
tree-hole up to 8 m. high and usually near water,
frequently perching in her search. In more open
country holes and crevices in banks and rocks or
under boulders are taken; as with Goldeneyes,
nestboxes are used and so are dark corners in
buildings. The same site may be used year after
year, and is lined with pale grey down in which
the 7 to 14 smooth, creamy eggs are laid, from
mid-March onwards in the south. The female
alone incubates, sometimes leaving her eggs to
join a mixed party on the water; they hatch in
4½ to 5 weeks. The downy ducklings, similar to
young Mergansers, with reddish cheeks, drop
from the nest a day or two later and are led away
by the female, who tends them until they fly at
5 to 6 weeks. They breed when 2 years old.

Male (left) and female (right)

Mergus albellus
SMEW
ANATIDAE Male 40 cm. (body: 25 cm.);
female smaller.

The smallest saw-bill has the most distinctive male plumage, the 'white nun' of wildfowlers, which becomes black and white in flight, showing the black back, and the blackish wing with dark speculum and white bar along the forewing. In eclipse (June to November) the male resembles the female but retains the black mantle and whiter wing. Juveniles are also like females, but their white wing-bars are less distinct. The males begin to show adult feathers about December, but do not attain full plumage until their second winter. The chestnut head should distinguish female and immature Smews from the smaller grebes at all seasons but confusion is possible under bad conditions of observation. On salt water the winter plumage of the Black Guillemot has some resemblance to that of the male Smew.

Unlike its larger relatives, the Smew is confined to Eurasia but with a comparatively small European breeding distribution in Scandinavia and western Russia, in wooded country some way from the sea. It migrates in autumn to southern Norway and Sweden, Denmark and the south coast of the Baltic, south-east Britain, then across western Europe to the Mediterranean, Balkans, Black and Caspian seas. The winter population of north-western Europe, on fresh waters and estuaries, is about 10,000 birds, of which up to 3000 may be in the Netherlands. 'Redheads' predominate in the south of the winter range.

Outside the breeding season Smews are usually seen in small parties, sometimes associating with other species, especially Goldeneyes to which they have a plumage resemblance and with which they are reported to have hybridized. They swim buoyantly except when alarmed and take off easily, almost springing off the water like Teal, *Anas crecca*, (B. W. Tucker) and have a rapid, noiseless flight, liable to sudden changes of direction. On long distances they adopt a line or V formation. They move without difficulty on land, running with upright carriage, perch freely in their wooded breeding habitat, and rest on the shore. They dive with speed but only stay under about 18 seconds, hunting small fish in both fresh and salt water. Wintering Smews watched by L. Nilsson in southern Sweden dived in shallow water, less than 2 m. deep. They also take crustaceans, small freshwater molluscs, worms and frogs. Mass-feeding by a large wintering flock has been observed in the Netherlands.

Smew display is described by P. A. Johnsgard as 'very energetic' and in this the female plays her part. Her inciting call is another, rattling variant of the diving ducks' harsh *krrr*, uttered at first quietly, then more loudly, with 'violent upward and forward body lunges', the bill stabbing downwards at each lunge; the whole performance is called 'bobbing' by P. A. D. Hollom. Attracted males swim ahead of the female, showing her the back of their heads with the 2 black marks. The male has ritualized comfort movements like stretching upwards and flapping the wings, but the most frequent and characteristic display is Hollom's 'pouting', when the head is laid smoothly along the back, with raising of the front feathers of the drooping crest. Pouting may take place on land though more usually on the water and is accompanied by a soft rattling call, also heard when the neck is stretched upward in a curiously formal movement. The sudden 'head-fling' may be an exaggerated form of pouting, with the forepart of the body raised at half a right angle out of the water and a louder rattling call. As with the Goosander, mutual 'drinking' is associated with mating but the female's prone position is different: her bill is laid on the water but the tail is raised. When mounted, the male flicks his wings a few times before swimming away from the female, who flings up her head, then may bathe or follow the male, 'bobbing' as she goes. Smews wintering in Sweden began communal courtship in late January; they were not seen actually mating until a month later (Nilsson).

The Smew is another tree-hole nester and, with the Goldeneye, one of the original nestbox birds in Lapland, though it was not encouraged as its eggs were not considered so palatable. The chosen hole was usually close to water and is lined with small tufts of very pale grey, white-centred down. Laying is from mid-May to mid-June and the usual clutch is 6 to 9 smooth, creamy to buff eggs, which hatch after 26 to 30 days incubation by the female. The ducklings show a contrasting down pattern: blackish upper parts and white below, with a black cap, white cheeks and throat and white on the wings. The female leads them to water and looks after them until they fledge when about 10 weeks old. They probably breed first at 2 years old.

The North American Hooded Merganser, *Mergus cucullatus*, about 46 cm. in total length, the male with a striking black-fringed white erectile 'hood' or crest, has been recorded twice in Britain and three times in Ireland. Johnsgard considers that it provides a link between the mergansers and the goldeneyes.

Female (bottom) and male (centre);
immature male (top)

Tadorna tadorna
SHELDUCK
ANATIDAE 60 cm. (body: 40 cm.)

The shelducks form a link between geese and typical ducks. Their heads look duck-like and they have 2 body moults a year; but the sexes are virtually identical in appearance and the males take a more gander-like part in family duties. The female Shelduck (lower bird opposite) is a little smaller and duller than the male, and lacks the conspicuous knob at the base of the bill. Both sexes have a not very pronounced eclipse plumage, acquired after the moult migration in July, a muted version of the full plumage, with some white on face and throat and a much duller chestnut breast band. Juveniles do not have the chest band and are dark grey-brown on the upper parts and head, with a white face and throat; their legs and bills are grey. By late autumn immature birds look like dull adults and by late winter some look fully adult, although they do not breed until 2 years old, some males not until they are 4 or 5 (J. Hori).

The first of several curious features of the Shelduck's habits and ecology is its breeding distribution. There is a mainly littoral range in north-western Europe: Britain and Ireland, the North Sea coasts and western Norway, Denmark and the western Baltic. There are several small enclaves round the Mediterranean and in Hungary and a larger one centred on the Crimea. Finally from the Caspian Sea eastward and southward there is the largest area of all, entirely inland. How this scatter came about is a zoogeographer's puzzle, but the Mediterranean enclaves are linked to the north-western range by winter visitors all down the coasts of France and Iberia. The north-western birds also have a moult migration, only described comparatively recently. In June and July the males, with most of the breeding females and the non-breeding birds, collect on the Knechtsand, a great area of mud and sand on the North Sea coast of Germany. Many of them travel overland to it and it was the discovery of a route across the English Pennines by R. A. H. Coombes and others that really exposed the whole story. Counts of 80,000 to 90,000 birds, estimated at 90 per cent of the total population, have been made at the Knechtsand by G. Goethe and H. Oelke. One mystery is the method by which some adult females are selected to stay behind with the young of the year. The gathering remains until the moult is over, then slowly disperses in September. Some birds of western origin return to their breeding area but others and the Baltic birds effect a true migration to the coasts of western Europe. There is a second, much smaller moult gathering in Bridgwater Bay, Somerset, which forms after the local Shelduck have left for the Knechtsand and may be composed, according to M. A. Ogilvie, of Irish birds. He has also assembled recent breeding population figures: 2500 to 5000 pairs for Britain, 2500 to 3000 in the Netherlands

and about 2000 pairs in the two Germanies. Shelduck are increasing and the winter population of north-western Europe may be 100,000 to 120,000 birds.

Their striking plumage and upright carriage make Shelduck easy to see, whether they are an isolated pair or, as more usually, a loose aggregation. Although they often swim, they spend most of their time on land, where they are completely at home. They tend to follow the tide when feeding, wading, dipping their heads or upending like 'dabbling' ducks. Their main prey is marine shellfish, especially *Hydrobium ulvae*; they also eat small crustaceans, insects, worms, small fish and their eggs, some seaweeds and parts of land plants. Shelduck fly readily, with rather slow wing-beats. The female's loud, diverlike, quacking call may be heard from birds on the wing over the salt marshes or sand dunes, perhaps *en route* to a freshwater pool to rest and preen. On long flights they fall into line or V formation.

Shelduck may pair for life, but this does not inhibit their range of displays. The female may incite her mate to attack another male by a ritualized 'pointing' of the bill with her neck stretched, uttering a call rendered *gaaa*. When he returns from the fray, he often 'preens' behind the wing, to which she responds, both of them exposing the metallic speculum which, whatever its original function, now has a significance in courtship. The male has a melodious, finch-like whistle (P. A. Johnsgard). This is given in various postures: when he is holding his neck straight and head still, when he is rotating it as a preliminary to attack, or in the remarkable head-flick, which ends with the bill held vertically upward. There is also a curious movement which Johnsgard calls the 'whistle-shake' and which occurs throughout the year and may have an alarm function. Females shake, but less vehemently and without calling. Both birds dip their heads in the water before mating, and the female bathes immediately afterwards.

Although Shelduck generally breed by the sea in north-western Europe, there are colonies by several Swedish lakes and pairs have nested many kilometres up English rivers; the 'colony' embraces territorial pairs, others awaiting territories and non-breeders. The nest is hidden, typically in a rabbit burrow but also under dense vegetation such as brambles, in hollow trees, under boulders, even in buildings, and may be 3 m. from daylight. Laying begins in early May and the 8 to 15 creamy eggs are surrounded by pale greyish-brown down. They hatch in 28 to 30 days, incubated only by the female though the male stays in the vicinity and usually helps guard the ducklings in their striking brown and white down. If the nest is far from water, the family makes a hazardous journey to a suitable shore. Here broods may combine under the care of a few females while the others leave on their moult migration. The young dive if attacked, a faculty not exercised by the adults. They are fledged at about 8 weeks.

Female (below) and male (above)

Anser species

GREY GEESE

ANATIDAE

Apart from the Snow Goose, *A. caerulescens*, a very rare visitor (or escape) from North America, and the Bar-headed Goose, *A. indicus*, which has been introduced to parts of Sweden, 5 species breed and all may be seen in winter in coastal areas, though not usually on open shores.

The Greylag Goose, *A. anser*, is the largest, 76 to 90 cm. long with a body of 48 to 50 cm., and best known. To the general grey goose pattern – grey-brown with a light-edged body feathers, white tail coverts and a white-tipped grey tail – are added the heavy head and orange bill, a pale grey forewing and grey rump. There are scattered black spots on the under parts, but not on juveniles, which may have greyish rather than pink legs.

The European breeding distribution is hard to define. Wild populations nest in Iceland, the Faeroe Islands (sporadic), north-west Scotland, the outer and Baltic coasts of Scandinavia, parts of Germany, Poland and western Russia. But the British and continental range has been greatly increased by released birds which may now live ferally or remain semi-tame. The northern areas are deserted in autumn and birds winter coastally and inland in many parts of Europe.

Ancestors of farmyard geese, Greylags resemble them in their gregariousness, loud honking call and threatening hiss. But they fly with ease, the wing-beats deceptively slow-looking; the V formation is usual on long flights. Greylags are vegetarian, gleaners and grazers. Their various displays were described by O. Heinroth, who emphasized the close pair bond. The gander who repels an enemy returns to his mate with the resonant 'triumph note', neck stretched and head close to ground. Mutual displays precede and follow mating in the water. Breeding may be solitary or colonial, on islands, moors, tundra, in reedbeds and marshes: in wet sites a large nest may be built. Down is sparsely used as lining for the 4 to 6 creamy eggs, which hatch after 4 weeks incubation by the goose. The goslings, in yellowish down at first, fly after 2 months but spend their first winter with their parents.

The Bean Goose, *A. fabalis*, is 70 to 76 cm. long with a body of 46 to 50 cm., the darkest species, but with conspicuous pale feather edges on the upper parts. Rather long-necked and slender, the Bean has orange-yellow legs and a variably black and orange bill. The European breeding area is in northern Scandinavia and Russia and the main winter quarters are in

southern Europe. Like its relatives it is vegetarian and sociable, but rather silent, its call resembling the Greylag's as do its displays and general breeding habits. It nests in open forest as well as on the tundra, beginning to lay in early June in the south of its range.

The Pink-footed Goose, *A. brachyrhynchus*, has been regarded as a western race of the Bean Goose. It is 60 to 76 cm. in total length with a body of 43 to 48 cm. Special features are the contrast between the dark head and neck and the grey-brown body, the pale forewing, the relatively small and stubby black bill with a pink band, and the pink legs. In winter it looks greyer than in summer; juveniles are darker than adults. The Pink-foot breeds in east Greenland, Iceland and Svalbard and winters mainly round the North Sea coast. Its call is between those of the Greylag and White-front in pitch. The diet is vegetarian and varied, including waste grain in winter; after feeding, flocks may roost on sandy coasts and estuaries. The colonial breeding sites are usually on ledges in rocky gorges; breeding begins in early June, conforming in general with other grey geese.

The White-fronted Goose, *A. albifrons*, is about 66 to 76 cm. in length, with a body 43 to 48 cm. Adults are distinguished by their dark plumage, white frontal blaze and black-barred breasts, a feature most prominent in the Greenland race *flavirostris*. Bills are variably pink to yellow; juveniles have yellow bills, no blaze, and unmarked underparts. White-fronts are marginally European breeders on the Russian north coast, but the range extends eastwards to west Greenland, whose small population migrates across the Atlantic to Britain and Ireland for the winter. The typical race winters over much of Europe. In general habits White-fronts resemble their relatives, but their laughing call is quite distinctive. Breeding, on tundra bogs and islands, begins in mid-June.

The Lesser White-fronted Goose, *A. erythropus*, is about 53 to 66 cm. long with a body 41 to 43 cm. It is distinguished from its relative by smaller size and bill, more extensive white blaze and a conspicuous yellow eye ring; the wings at rest project beyond the tail. Its feeding actions are also noticeably faster. Juveniles lack blaze and barred under parts but show the eye ring. The Scandinavian breeding area includes much high ground and extends eastwards to the Russian tundra. In winter this is a rare visitor to Britain, but occurs from France eastwards. The high-pitched call can be told in a flock from that of the White-front, with which it is often associated. Breeding begins at the end of May in drier sites than those chosen by its relatives.

Pink-footed Goose (*top*), *Bean Goose* (*centre left*),
White-fronted Goose (*centre right*),
and Greylag Goose (*bottom*)

Branta bernicla
BRENT GOOSE

ANATIDAE 56 to 60 cm. (body: 41 to 43 cm.)

Four 'black' geese may occur on the coasts of Northern Europe, the 3 species described here and the small (about 53 cm.) Red-breasted Goose, *B. ruficollis*, a straggler from its nearest wintering area by the Black Sea, more often an escape from wildfowl collections. The 3 races of Brent Geese are distinguishable in the field: the dark-breasted *bernicla* breeds in the arctic archipelagos of Europe and in Siberia; the pale-breasted *hrota* breeds in Svalbard, Greenland and arctic Canada; and the black-breasted *nigricans*, sometimes regarded as a separate species, breeds in Alaska and Siberia and has occasionally turned up in Europe.

Brent show no visible differences between summer and winter plumage: all races have black heads, necks and upper breasts, dark grey upper parts with light feather margins, and black tails framed by white tail coverts. The three races are typically distinguished by their under parts, though there may be individual variation. Juveniles lack the small white patches on the sides of the neck and the black is duller; in the first winter and summer, areas of the wing show white-tipped feathers.

The dark-breasted Brent has a world population estimated at about 75,000, of which about half winter in Britain. After breeding, the birds migrate through Russia, Scandinavia and Germany to the North Sea coasts and as far south as the Mediterranean. The tiny pale-breasted Svalbard population of about 200 birds winters in Denmark and in north-east England. The main pale-breasted population, from Greenland, winters chiefly in Ireland; some Canadian birds may also cross the Atlantic.

Most consistently littoral of European geese, Brent are associated with beds of the green eelgrass *Zostera* and the birds, which flock closely at all times, may be seen as a black mass at low tide, busily pulling up the plants by the roots. They also feed on seaweeds, especially the green *Enteromorpha*, and some shellfish and crustaceans. When pressed, they may graze above the tideline and on the breeding grounds they take grasses and other land plants. Between bouts of feeding, and when roosting, the flocks retire offshore. The croaking call, single or 2-syllabled, contrasts with the honking of other geese. In flight they prefer wavy lines to the V formation, usually keeping low over the water.

An aggressive Brent thrusts its head forward, exposing the white neck patches, and hisses. The white tail coverts are used in display and as contact signals. The gander chases his mate through the air over the breeding area and there are mutual displays on the ground at mating. The colonial nesting places are on islands or close to the shore; laying over most of the range begins in June; the usual clutch of 4 elongated, cream to yellow eggs is laid in an open nest hollow, lined with the goose's dark down. She sits for about 4 weeks, the gander in attendance. When the grey downy goslings hatch, he helps her look after them and the family stays together over the winter.

Branta leucopsis
BARNACLE GOOSE

ANATIDAE 58 to 70 cm. (body: 43 to 46 cm.)

Unlike the Brent, the Barnacle Goose has no subspecies and a much more limited range. Although the crown, nape, neck and upper breast are glossy black, it looks much lighter than its relative, with pale grey under parts, upper parts predominantly grey with black and white bars, and the striking creamy face and forehead. The sexes are alike in winter and summer; the juvenile has a pale grey face, flanks more barred, and a brownish tinge to the mantle.

The only known breeding places of the Barnacle Goose are 2 coastal areas of east Greenland, Svalbard, Novaya Zemlya and the coast of west Siberia. Greenland birds winter in northwest Britain and Ireland, the Svalbard population of about 5000 by the Solway Firth in southwest Scotland, and the Siberian element on the coasts of the North Sea and Baltic.

Barnacle Geese are grazers, on coastal grassland in winter and on the sparse vegetation of the breeding areas. They are considered to be relatively approachable and, while they normally stay in flocks, odd birds or groups may be found with other species. On the wing they favour the V formation, uttering the chorus which reminded B. W. Tucker of the 'shrill yelping of a pack of small terriers'. Before flying they show off their white faces by movements of the head and neck. During the 'triumph ceremony' members of a pair call shrilly and the wings are flapped alternately. There is a mutual head-dipping display before mating.

In Svalbard the Barnacle nests mainly in loose colonies on offshore islands, or on rock bastions above valleys, often using the same nest hollow year after year, lining it with the dark-grey, white-centred down. The 3 to 6 creamy white eggs are laid from late May and hatch after about 3½ weeks, incubated by the goose with the gander in attendance. The goslings fly in 7 weeks, but stay with the parents for their first winter.

Branta canadensis
CANADA GOOSE

ANATIDAE 90 to 102 cm. (body: 53 to 60 cm.)

This is the largest of the 'black' geese, though in fact its body plumage resembles that of a grey goose, only the head and neck being black with a broad white chinstrap. It is now a well-established introduction to Britain, parts of Ireland

and south Sweden, whence it migrates in winter across the Baltic. Odd birds also cross the Atlantic from its native continent where there are a dozen subspecies. Canada Geese are seldom seen on the open coast but may nest by estuaries and visit them in flocks outside the breeding season. In Britain the Yorkshire population has developed an annual moult migration to the Beauly Firth in north-east Scotland.

In foreground, two Barnacle Geese; in background, the light (left) and dark (right) races of Brent Goose

Haematopus ostralegus
OYSTERCATCHER
HAEMATOPODIDAE 43 cm., including bill.

Picturesquely called the Sea-pie, the Oyster-catcher is a conspicuous bird with a conspicuous nest, yet is highly successful in terms of numbers and distributional spread. The pied plumage, which includes a broad white wing-bar and rump above a black terminal tail band, sets off the adult's orange-red bill and pink legs; the sexes are alike. The juvenile is duller, mottled brown above, with a dark tip to the bill and greyish legs. It also shows a narrow white half-collar. This is an indication of non-breeding (smaller figures on plate), not only of immaturity and is seen generally in autumn and winter flocks. The red-rimmed eye of the adult is red; the juvenile's eye is brown.

The small world-wide family of oystercatchers has recently been divided by P. B. Heppleston into 5 species, of which *ostralegus* is given 16 races, 3 of them in Northern Europe and one occupying, like the Shelduck, a huge inland range in central Asia. Iceland and the Faeroe Islands are the home of the race *malacophaga*, Britain and Ireland of *occidentalis*, while the typical *ostralegus* breeds coastally from north-western Russia all the way to Gibraltar, with enclaves in the Mediterranean. European Oystercatchers are partly resident, partly migratory from the north, and very large wintering flocks may form, for example in the Netherlands and in the estuaries of Britain, where there were nearly 200,000 birds in September 1972.

Running about grassland with wings slightly raised, standing in black masses on the shore, or in rather fluttering flight with loud *kleep kleep* calls, Oystercatchers are a good example of a wader that scorns camouflage (though a bird sitting among boulders and dead seaweed may be hard to see). There are 2 distinct feeding methods, for both of which the powerful, slightly bulbous, laterally compressed bill is well adapted. They probe in soil or mud for worms and insect larvae, and they attack molluscs from limpets to mussels and cockles, opening bivalves either *in situ* or after removal, to strike at the point of weakness. A. J. Drinnan has calculated that in North Wales one bird in winter eats its own weight of wet shellfish a day. Predation on cockles has therefore economic repercussions and 7000 Oystercatchers were killed in South Wales in 1973–4, an action strongly opposed by conservationists.

The best known of the Oystercatcher's displays is the 'piping performance', indicating excitement. Two, 3 or more birds stretch their necks forward with rounded shoulders, point their bills downward and open them to emit a prolonged series of speeded-up *kleeps*, merging into a trill and slowing down again perhaps several times. This usually takes place during a ritualized run, but also in the air, even from a perch; most often it concerns territorial rights (Heppleston). The male also has a butterfly flight, and mating is surrounded by elaborate ceremonies.

The breeding habitat of the Oystercatcher was originally coastal: stony shingle or sandy beaches, maritime turf, and low rocky headlands and islands. Fairly recently there has been a considerable spread inland in parts of north-western Europe from the Netherlands to Denmark and south Sweden, but most noticeably in Scotland and northern England where pairs, moving up river valleys, may nest 600 m. up on river shingle, fields, moorland, burnt ground, even open woodland. Nest scrapes may persist for years, lined afresh with pebbles, shells, rabbit pellets and plant stems. Both sexes 'build', and incubate the 2 to 4 large buff to stone-coloured eggs with dark spots and scrawls. These are laid from late March in the south of the range and hatch in 24 to 27 days. The downy young, dark and buff above, white below, leave the nest after a day or two and fledge in about 5 weeks. The parents are vociferous in their defence and will 'buzz' intruders.

OPPOSITE *In foreground, summer adult; behind, non-breeding birds*
BELOW *Adult Lapwing*

Vanellus vanellus
LAPWING or PEEWIT
CHARADRIIDAE 30 cm.

This, the best known wader over much of Northern Europe, belongs to the round-winged group of plovers. Black and white at a distance, on close view the Lapwing in spring shows beautifully iridescent upper parts and a curved crest, more pronounced on the male, who also has broader wings. Juveniles show a suffusion of brownish buff, white throats and short crests,

RAYMOND WATSON

and winter adults rather resemble them. The eyes are brown, bill black and legs brownish pink. The Lapwing breeds in a broad band across Eurasia from Ireland to the Pacific. There is a shift of population in autumn and in hard weather, from north-east to south-west and from inland coastwards.

Lapwings flock in parties of 10 to 10,000 or more, often frequent muddy shores where the birds bunch when resting, spread out to feed. Running a few paces, they tilt forward to pick out worms or insect larvae; at times they are victimized by gulls. In flight Lapwings waver and twinkle in loose clouds. The male's twisting display flight with its wing music and 5-note song is as well known as the *pee-wit* call. The male shows off the chestnut under tail coverts when scrape-forming. Lapwings breed from 900 m. to sea level on marshes and beaches, laying 4 pear-shaped brown eggs, often heavily blotched, in a well-lined nest from March onwards. The downy young hatch after about 4 weeks' incubation by both parents and leave the nest at once. Tended mainly by the female, they fledge in $4\frac{1}{2}$ to 5 weeks, but both parents demonstrate in their defence.

Charadrius hiaticula
RINGED PLOVER
CHARADRIIDAE 19 cm.

One of the most widespread and typical birds of Northern Europe's low-lying shores, the Ringed Plover is vulnerable, in its preferred breeding haunts, to the human holiday explosion at the seaside in summer. In fact it may still try to carry out its traditional role despite children, dogs and beachballs, relying on its concealing plumage to give it some immunity. The sexes are substantially alike, but the female tends to be dark brown rather than black on the head and neck both in summer and winter. The juvenile is even browner; the pale margins to its back feathers give it a scaly appearance and the less defined head pattern approaches that of the Kentish Plover which, however, has blackish legs in all plumages, whereas the Ringed Plover's are yellowish, unless muddied. In flight the white wing-bar separates this species from the Little Ringed Plover, but is not a reliable distinction from the Kentish Plover which has a narrower band.

The Ringed Plover's breeding range is circumpolar or mainly Eurasian, according to the view taken on the status of the North American Semipalmated Plover, which K. H. Voous regards as a distinct species, *C. semipalmatus*, overlapping but not interbreeding with *C. hiaticula* in Greenland and arctic Canada. In Europe the Ringed Plover nests in Iceland, Svalbard, the Faeroe Islands, Britain and Ireland and eastward right round the coastline from Brittany to Russia and Siberia, including the Baltic, and penetrating inland in Scandinavia and parts of Britain, with enclaves far to the south on the Continent. In winter there is a general move south, many birds reaching the tropics and even extreme southern Africa, while others may be sedentary; but recent research suggests that some birds passing through Britain in August have bred in Greenland (G. H. Green).

The tubby form and twinkling feet of the Ringed Plover may often be seen mingled with other small waders, especially Dunlin. But plovers feed distinctively, tilting the whole body downward to seize their often minute prey, unlike the continual probing of their long-billed companions. When alarmed, the dispersed foragers gather with their piping *tooi* and quiet *trrrp* calls and take off in a bunch, perhaps circling back, after flying low over the sea, to feed again. They take a variety of small molluscs and crustaceans, marine worms and, in the wrack line and higher, a variety of insects.

The aerial chase between several birds is accompanied by a trilling song composed of speeded-up call notes; there is also a stiff-winged 'slow-motion' display flight. On the ground the male puffs himself up in front of the female, showing off the black collar; he also, like many other waders, performs ritualized nest-scraping actions. Ringed Plovers breed in a variety of habitats, from the typical sandy and pebbly shores to marine turf and low rocky slabs; inland they are found on river and lakeside shingle, gravel pits, stony 'brecks', arable land, as well as tundra moorland to high altitudes in Scandinavia. The nest scrape may be lined with pebbles, small shells and plant fragments and is usually quite open, sometimes sheltered by a grass tuft, occasionally hidden. The 4 stone-coloured eggs, spotted and scrawled with black, are laid from March onwards in the south, more generally in May and June. Both sexes incubate them, with frequent changes-over, for 3½ weeks. The downy chicks are active at once and fledge in 3½ to 4 weeks. At the nest or when with young, the adults may put on a vigorous distraction display with spread tail and fluttering wings. There are 2, occasionally 3 broods. Sometimes several pairs may nest among a colony of Little Terns.

Charadrius alexandrinus
KENTISH PLOVER
CHARADRIIDAE 16 cm.

This smaller, more delicate, less boldly marked species is the southern 'replacer' of the Ringed Plover, with which it may compete, apparently unsuccessfully. The relatively long, blackish legs distinguish it at all times from its northern rival and from the Little Ringed Plover, though juveniles of these species have similar less defined head and neck patterns. Males in breeding plumage show a pronounced rufous tint to the crown. The breeding distribution is almost world-wide from about 50°N to 40°S, and, while mainly coastal, includes a large inland area in central Asia. In Northern Europe it breeds from Brittany eastward to Denmark, but has not been proved to nest in England since 1956. The winter picture is confused, but the North European population is migratory and small flocks may form in autumn before departure south.

The Kentish Plover is a smaller, more active version of the Ringed Plover, with a diagnostic *wit-wit-wit* call and a trilling song, uttered in 'bat-like, wavering' display flight (B. W. Tucker). The food in summer is largely insects and their larvae, spiders, small molluscs, crustaceans and worms. The breeding habitat is usually sandy or shingly and the 3 eggs, similar to the Ringed Plover's but often more streaked, are laid from May onwards in a shallow scrape in which they are often more or less buried when the bird leaves. Incubation, by both parents, lasts 3½ weeks; the fledging period is about the same and there may be 2 broods. In Denmark Kentish Plovers sometimes nest in association with Avocets (T. Dybbro).

The Little Ringed Plover, *C. dubius*, of wide Eurasian distribution, sometimes visits sandy and shingly sea shores. It is distinguished from the 2 previous species by lack of a wing-bar and by the prominent orange eye ring.

*In foreground, Ringed Plover adult (below) and
juvenile (above); in background, Kentish Plover adult
(above) and juvenile (below)*

Pluvialis squatarola
GREY PLOVER
CHARADRIIDAE 28 cm.

Described by K. H. Voous as 'one of the greatest migrants among the world's migratory birds', the Grey Plover is also one of the few species selected for major treatment in this book which barely nests within the confines of Northern Europe. So it is in winter plumage that most observers become familiar with it, looking superficially like a rather large Golden Plover until it takes wing, when the black axillaries of the underwing (the coverts are whitish) show up in all their clinching definition, the whitish rump, tail and wing-bar being additional features. At close range the dark bars across the tail become visible. Seen at rest, the adults' grey-brown upper parts are less mottled than those of the Golden Plover, but juveniles look very like their near relatives and identification may have to wait until they take wing. The under parts of both adults and juveniles are very pale ash-brown to white on the belly and vent. In summer – the plumage may be seen on both spring and autumn passage – the male is magnificent, his upper parts spangled black and white, divided from the deep black face, throat and upper breast by the white forehead and side of neck; the belly remains white. The female has white tips to the feathers of her upper parts, including the wing-coverts; her under parts are less deeply black than the male's and are flecked with white; the white under tail coverts have brown markings. By their first summer both sexes are almost as adults, with traces of golden brown on wings and rump. Unlike the Golden and Ringed Plovers, the Grey Plover has a small hind toe.

'Arctic' summarizes the Grey Plover's breeding distribution: a rather narrow band following the coast from Kanin and Kolguev in northern Russia east to the Bering Strait and thence over to Alaska and Canada's Baffin Island and Southampton Island. After breeding, the birds spread southwards on an almost world-wide basis down to 40°S. Large numbers of non-breeders remain for the summer in some areas, for example, East Africa, where they are quite regular on inland waters. Most of the Grey Plovers seen in Northern Europe are therefore on passage, though British and Irish estuaries held over 9000 birds in January 1973.

Grey Plovers behave like slightly sedate Golden Plovers. They can often be picked out as scattered individuals standing up among a host of smaller waders on the shore, though they may come together as a party on taking wing, when they fly as fast and purposefully as their relatives. They are usually seen on muddy estuaries and beaches, feeding on worms, small molluscs and crustaceans, with some insects and plant seeds when they venture inland. Studying North American passage migrants in Connecticut, M. C. Baker found that polychaete worms,

especially *Nereis succinea*, were the favourite prey both in spring and autumn. They were grasped by one end and pulled out of the mud; clams were gripped by their siphons, and very small morsels were swallowed immediately after capture. The prey was sometimes dunked in shallow water, probably to clean it.

The call is most often heard from parties on the wing, a 3-syllabled *tlee-oo-ee*, sometimes shortened to *tlooee*. A more mellow note is uttered on the ground as well and there is a tern-like alarm call which, with other notes, is heard on the breeding ground. Here the males perform a dazzling display flight involving a deep dive and upward recovery, several taking part together; hovering and 'slow-motion' flight actions are also described, and the male may display on the ground.

The barest tundra is the Grey Plover's chosen breeding habitat, with a preference for stony ridges. Here the nest scrape is made in the almost prostrate vegetation, usually with a good view, and lined with local plant fragments. The 4 eggs, laid in the second half of June in north Russia, have a very variable ground-colour, generally light buff but ranging from pinkish to greenish, and are spotted and blotched at the broadest part with dark brown, often forming a zone. Both sexes incubate the clutch, which hatches in 23 days. The downy young are golden-buff above with a pronounced white collar and under parts; they leave the nest when dry and feed themselves, tended by the parents, who put on exaggerated injury-feigning displays if disturbed when on the nest or with the brood, flicking their wings or crouching with wings and tail spread (male watched by A. Trevor-Battye).

Eudromias morinellus
DOTTEREL
CHARADRIIDAE 22 cm.

A smaller brown-backed plover which may sometimes be seen on the coast when on passage is the Dotterel, a nesting species traditionally of the arctic–alpine zone which has recently taken to breeding on land reclaimed from the sea in the Netherlands. It is darker on the back than the Grey and Golden Plovers and the stripe over the eye, so prominent in summer, is obscured in winter plumage. The under parts shade from brown on the breast and flanks to white on the belly, with traces of the summer white stripe across the breast still visible. The legs are yellowish, bill black, and eyes brown.

Dotterel travel in 'trips', from a few birds to a dozen or more, and are likely to be seen above the tideline, on sandy links and fields. Their calls include a soft peeping note and a 3-syllabled whistle, likely to be uttered when the birds take wing. But they are usually absurdly tame. The food on passage includes small molluscs, worms and some plant matter.

Grey Plover in summer (bottom) and in winter plumage (centre)

Pluvialis apricaria
GOLDEN PLOVER
CHARADRIIDAE 28 cm.

Although not so much of a shore bird as the Grey Plover in winter and on passage, the Golden Plover is quite likely to be found on muddy estuaries and coastlines and open ground near the sea, sometimes in large flocks. Two races breed in Northern Europe but they are not to be distinguished in the field in winter. The gold and black upper parts are characteristic at all seasons, though juvenile Grey Plovers and the very rare Lesser Golden Plover, *P. dominica*, from North America and Asia can cause confusion. The under parts of the Golden Plover in winter are white with golden-yellow and dark markings, mainly on the throat, breast and flanks; the important distinctions are the whitish axillaries (black on Grey Plover and smoky grey on Lesser Golden Plover), the lack of a distinct wing-bar and the dark appearance of the rump and tail in flight (though this feature is shared with the Lesser Golden Plover). In summer the under parts of both sexes of the southern race *apricaria* become blackish, and the face becomes dusky. There is no clear delimitation between the under parts and the spangled black and gold upper parts. A typical male of the northern race *altifrons* is as black as a Grey Plover from face to belly, with a clear white border between the black and upper parts. The female is almost as resplendent, but the white border is often less well marked, and intermediates between the 2 races are common. Juveniles are like winter adults with somewhat paler upper parts and darker under parts.

Compared with the Lesser Golden Plover, which is obviously a very close relative, this species has a restricted breeding range. The northern race nests in Iceland, the Faeroe Islands, northern Scandinavia, the Baltic states and Russia, eastward into Siberia where it meets *P. dominica* and apparently may hybridize with it. The southern race breeds in Britain, Ireland and southern Scandinavia but is now rare in Germany. Males or pairs of the northern race are reported from time to time as breeding in Britain and it is doubtful whether a firm line can be drawn between the 2 forms. After breeding, the higher inland and northern haunts are deserted and wintering birds reach south-western Europe and north-western Africa, being seen in between on passage both in spring and autumn. Franz Sauer considers that the modern migration routes are of very ancient origin, from glacial times; for example, that which Siberian birds follow to the Netherlands by way of the Baltic. Ringing recoveries strongly suggest that the Icelandic breeding population winters predominantly in Ireland, with smaller numbers in Britain.

On passage or in winter flocks of Golden Plovers usually keep to themselves or mix with Lapwings: when disturbed the 2 species separate in the air, the flashing knife-winged movements of the Golden Plover contrasting with the relatively lumbering flight of the round-winged Lapwing. They feed in the usual plover run, stop, tilt forward style, taking a great variety of adult and larval insects, with small molluscs, crustaceans, earth and marine worms and spiders. Grass, seeds and other plant matter are also eaten. When resting, birds often raise one or both wings, the white undersides showing up suddenly in the concourse of rounded golden-brown bodies. Once alerted, their stance is upright.

The common call is a musical *too-ee*, often heard in flight and used at all seasons. On the breeding grounds there is a much larger vocabulary, and D. Nethersole-Thompson describes 2 songs, one uttered in slow, flapping display flight by one or several males, at heights up to 300 m. in the air: a remarkably mournful *per-pee-oo per-pee-oo*, accented on the middle syllable. The

OPPOSITE *Adults in summer, northern race (below) and southern race (above)*
ABOVE *Adult in winter*

other, a rippling *too-roo too-roo*, appears to indicate excitement in various situations and may be heard from flocks on the wing. On the territory the watchful off-nest bird gives a single plaintive *too*, repeated at intervals as, running from eminence to eminence, it dogs the human intruder. Several other calls are associated with stages in the breeding cycle.

The males fight for females and for display centres; there is also much chasing of females by one or more males. After pairing, the birds become comparatively quiet and feed together, with occasional outbursts of mutual aggression;

there seems to be no conspicuous display before mating. The male initiates scrape-forming, the female choosing and lining one with grass stems and other local material. The breeding habitat varies from arctic and alpine tundra to disintegrating bogs, moorland, burnt ground, grass moors, even open woodland. The nest is usually exposed, sometimes partly sheltered by a tussock. The 4 creamy-buff eggs, beautifully blotched at the broad end with dark browns, are laid from the end of March in the south and incubated mainly by the female. They hatch in 4 to nearly 5 weeks and the chicks may take up to 100 hours to break out of the egg; they stay in the nest for 24 to 36 hours unless disturbed. Bright, almost metallic yellow and black above, whitish below, they harmonize wonderfully with lichens and mosses and are guarded by both parents until they fledge in about 4 weeks. Nethersole-Thompson has distinguished 7 forms of distraction display used by the adults, most of them giving the impression of injury, especially to the wings, though one is a fluttering flight and another a 'rodent-run' through the vegetation; the male may also run towards the cause of disturbance.

Arenaria interpres
TURNSTONE
CHARADRIIDAE 23 cm.

The turnstones are a very small and puzzling group, placed by some authorities with the plovers, although they have a well-developed hind toe, by others in the Scolopacidae with the long-billed waders. Their outstanding feature is the rather short, conical bill. The Turnstone's summer plumage is also quite distinctive, its upper parts usually described as tortoise-shell, with black and white patterning on head and neck and round the tail. The summer female is not as bright or clear-cut in colour as the male, but the sexes are alike in winter, with generally dusky-brown upper parts. Juveniles resemble them but are even duller, with yellowish-brown legs. Transitional plumages are often seen on passage birds. In flight Turnstones show a crescentic black patch on the otherwise white rump, with a broad black subterminal band on the white-tipped tail, a white wing-bar, and white shoulder patches.

This is another primarily arctic breeding species, with a relict population in the Baltic. Otherwise it breeds round the northern coasts of Eurasia and America, with a gap in north-east Canada, south Greenland and Iceland (where it breeds occasionally). The arctic American race *morinella* is one of the most northerly breeding waders, recorded at 83°N in Greenland. The only other species, the Black Turnstone, *A. melanocephala*, is more or less confined to coastal Alaska. Turnstones spend the summer in many places outside their normal breeding range, which has led to speculation that they may have bred, for example, in Scotland. Their autumn migration takes them right beyond the tropics to Argentina, South Africa and New Zealand and to occupy a variety of maritime habitats with rock or stones as common denominators. Even far south, birds may be seen in summer plumage, which is attained in the first year, though Turnstones do not breed until 2 years old. On passage they cross the Eurasian continent and the North Atlantic. They also travel fast: a Heligoland-ringed bird was shot 800 km. away in France 25 hours after release.

To those who know them mainly on passage or in winter Turnstones are essentially waders of the rocky coast, including man's rock-like artefacts, piers and breakwaters; their companions are Purple Sandpipers, Redshanks, Dunlins, and on beaches Sanderlings. Usually in small parties, they search the hanging seaweed rapidly, tossing the fronds aside. Then they blossom from dun into pied as they take wing low over the water with their twittering call notes, perhaps to land on a stony beach, where they start living up to their names. There are instances of apparent cooperation between several birds in turning over a large object. Their diet is extraordinarily varied, even if in winter it is mainly small crustaceans and molluscs. They will feed on carrion and scavenge damaged shellfish (R. E. Jones), including bivalve shells they have opened them. In summer Göran Bergman has recorded them piercing the eggs of gulls, terns, ducks, and their own species on the Baltic islands. In arctic Canada they scrounged round the camps of the men studying them. But their usual summer food is, first, seeds and other plant matter, then small spiders and moth larvae (caught by turning over 'plates' of dry mud) and finally the swarming insect life as it emerges.

Catholic as its eating habits may be, on vocabulary and display the Turnstone seems rather light. A 'song', sometimes heard on passage and used when excited, as in mobbing a predator, appears to be built up from the usual call note; there is also a single *keu* of alarm. According to D. N. Nettleship, pairs seem to form on migration or in groups on the beaches after arrival at Ellesmere Island. They then take up territories, which the male controls from a prominent stance, fighting off and chasing rivals and landless birds, in the air or on the ground. Over most of the range the habitat is bare ground: tundra, island turf caps, moorland or river flats some miles inland, but in the Baltic nests are often in thick cover and on wooded islands. The 3 to 4 eggs, with an olive-green ground and sometimes dense brown spotting, are laid from mid-May in the south and incubated from the first egg, at first mainly by the female; they hatch in 22 days. The downy chicks, buff and grey above, white below, leave the nest-scrape within 24 hours and are taken to a suitable pool where they can feed on chironomid flies. The female leaves them with the male in charge before fledging takes place at about 19 days. He then departs, and flocks of juveniles form on the beaches, migrating after the adults.

*Adult in summer (bottom), in transitional plumage
(centre left) and in winter (centre right)*

Numenius arquata
CURLEW
SCOLOPACIDAE 48 to 63·5 cm. (including bill: 10 to 15 cm., larger in females).

This largest of waders can, with its grey-brown blend, be taken in flight for an immature gull. The bill is about 3 times the length of the head, a distinguishing character from the shorter-billed Whimbrel. Close-up the subtle variation of light and dark brown in the plumage is apparent, the dark streaks petering out on the white belly; the whitish rump shades into the barred tail. The sexes are alike and their paler winter plumage is hardly discernible in the field. Juveniles have shorter bills and a plumage similar to but rather brighter than that of a summer adult.

The Curlew is a Eurasian bird with a range generally to the south of the Whimbrel, and there may be competition where they overlap. In Shetland they are neatly separated by altitude, Curlews occupying the valleys and lower ground. In Iceland they are only occasional visitors and the Whimbrel is supreme. The Curlew's breeding distribution runs from Ireland, Britain and Brittany east across Europe, roughly between 50°N and 60°N, but including the Baltic and the west coast of Norway and reaching south to the Black Sea. After breeding, there is a general move to the coasts and southward into Africa and southern Asia but many birds winter in the breeding area, withstanding hard weather. British and Irish estuaries held about 77,000 birds in September 1972 and about 54,500 in January 1973.

On the muddy, often estuarine shores that they prefer, Curlews may be seen individually, in scattered parties, or in flocks of hundreds. They mix with other waders, stalking majestically among the almost feverish activity of the smaller species, or resting like grey monuments when all are awaiting the ebb tide that will free the feeding grounds. The Curlew is a prober, whether in tidal mud or inland pastures and bogs: on the coast it takes shellfish, crustaceans, small fish and marine worms. Inland many insects are eaten, with earthworms, snails, slugs, small frogs, moorland berries and grass seeds, a varied diet for such an apparently specialized bill. Curlews wade frequently and swim when necessary. On the wing their slow beats enhance their resemblance to large gulls, especially when they fly in formation, but they plane down to land with a flutter of dark wing-tips. It is in flight that the Curlew's voice is most often heard, whether it is the variable *coor-lee* call, origin of its common name, or the sharp *whaup* which is the Scottish choice of common name. The celebrated 'song' warms up with a series of *coors* into the bubbling trill before dying away and then renewing itself as the bird, having mounted almost vertically, holds himself in the air, then glides downwards as he trills. The female can also bubble, and less complete versions are often heard on the shore. Displays on the breeding ground include the pair gliding side by side and a V-winged flight by the male (D. Nethersole-Thompson).

Males begin bubbling over prospective territories early in the season; these may be established on a variety of habitats from heather and grass moors, rough pastures and arable land to low-lying marshes, heaths, dunes, and even open woodland. The large, deep nest-scrape, lined with grasses, may be partly protected by a tussock of grass or heather but is sometimes quite exposed. Laying starts from mid-April in the south of the range and the 3 or 4 eggs may appear at intervals of about 2 days; they are broad, rather pointed and slightly glossy, greenish or brownish usually spotted rather than blotched with darker brown. The female takes the larger share in incubation, which begins when the clutch is complete. The downy, short-billed chicks are rich buff and dark brown above, paler buff below; they soon leave the nest and are tended by both parents at first, eventually by the male on his own. They fledge when 5 to 6 weeks old.

Numenius phaeopus
WHIMBREL
SCOLOPACIDAE 38 to 41 cm. (including bill: 9 cm.)

The Curlew's northern replacer is, against the rules, a rather smaller bird with a bill about twice the length of its head. Apart from this, the head pattern of 2 broad dark bands divided by a narrow pale stripe is quite distinctive if it can be seen. The upper parts are also rather darker than the Curlew's; on juveniles even more so.

The Whimbrel has a discontinuous breeding range; in Northern Europe this runs from Iceland to the Faeroe Islands, northern Scotland (especially Shetland) to western and northern Scandinavia, the Baltic states and eastward on a broad swathe into western Siberia. There is a completely separate area in east Siberia more or less connected with a mainly coastal belt in Alaska, which extends south-east across arctic Canada to Hudson Bay. In winter Whimbrels migrate almost as far south in all continents as is possible, even to Tierra del Fuego, and are seen on passage along the coasts of Northern Europe, in Britain more numerously in spring than in autumn, with about 3000 birds on the estuaries in May.

First evidence of the Whimbrel's presence on passage is often its 'seven whistles', a tittering series of notes which is generally diagnostic, although Curlews can utter something very like it. The birds usually travel in small parties, and land to feed on the shore where they behave much as Curlews but are said to be less wary. They probe for crustaceans, molluscs and worms; inland they also take many insects and later moorland berries. The male's display song, uttered in flight, closely resembles the Curlew's though there are apparently variations. There is a sharp alarm call, equivalent to the Curlew's *whaup*.

The breeding habitat is generally bare tundra or comparatively dry moorland; also rough grassland and birch tundra. The open nest scrape is sparsely lined for the 4 eggs, similar to but often more heavily marked than Curlew's. They are laid from late May onwards and incubated by both sexes. The downy chicks are like little Curlews but already show the dark bands on the crown; they hatch in about $3\frac{1}{2}$ weeks and are tended by both parents until fledging at about 4 weeks.

Adult Curlew in foreground, adult Whimbrel behind

83

Limosa limosa
BLACK-TAILED GODWIT

SCOLOPACIDAE 38 to 43 cm. (including bill: 9·5 to 12 cm.)

The godwits, like the curlews, form a small generic group within the great family of long-billed waders. The name has no sacred associations: it is said to refer to their 'good' eating qualities. This is slightly the larger of the 2 species occurring in North Europe and can be distinguished in flight from its relative at all seasons by the dark primaries and prominent white wing-bar, and by the white tail, below a dark rump, with its broad black terminal band and legs projecting well beyond. In fact, confusion in flight is more likely with an Oystercatcher or even a Redshank. On the ground the 2 godwits look more alike, but this species has longer legs and a slightly longer, almost straight bill. The chestnut of the summer plumage is less extensive than on the Bar-tailed Godwit and not so rich in colour; the larger female is usually paler than the male. There are irregular dark markings both on the back and on the white belly. But in winter the grey-brown back is darker and more uniform than the Bar-tail's and the under parts light grey instead of whitish. The pink bill shades into a dark tip on both species. Although the juvenile resembles a winter adult, its breast has a chestnut tinge recalling the summer plumage, a feature which recurs on other juvenile waders.

The Eurasian breeding range of the Black-tailed Godwit extends from Britain to the Sea of Okhotsk mainly between 50° and 60°N, but tilting northward at each extreme, to include Iceland with its own race islandica, and parts of north-eastern Siberia, home of the race melanuroides. Some American authorities have also grouped the scarce Hudsonian Godwit, L. haemastica, of north-western Canada within the species. The breeding habitats vary from bare moorland and dwarf willow scrub to lush meadows and sand dunes, the first 2 characteristic of the Iceland race, a few pairs of which breed in the Faeroe Islands and northern Scotland, the second 2 of the nominate race, which has recently recolonized areas in eastern England, evidently from the Netherlands, where the breeding population may sometimes approach 50,000 pairs. Migration after breeding or failing to breed begins in June and July, the main European population wintering from the Mediterranean southward into tropical Africa, with about 100,000 birds in the Niger inundation zone (F. Roux) and stragglers as far as South Africa, while the eastern race reaches Australia by way of South-east Asia. Recent counts suggest that some 70,000 birds winter in Europe (including Britain and Ireland) and North Africa and A. J. Prater considers that the majority of these are from Iceland, whose breeding population he puts at between 40,000 and 60,000 birds, representing a substantial increase in the past half century.

Stalking over grassland or muddy shore, the tall, long-necked Black-tailed Godwit makes small pecking movements, then suddenly bores into the ground or below the surface of shallow water, into which it often wades breast-deep, and pulls out its prey: a mollusc, worm, larval or adult insect. It also takes small fish and frog-spawn, with seeds of sedges and berries in its northern breeding grounds. Passage and wintering birds may be alone, in small parties, or large flocks, their drab upper parts blending with the shore until they burst into black and white on taking wing.

Flocks are not noted for their manoeuvres in the air as are those of the Bar-tail, but they frequently call a repeated whicka whicka, also used as an alarm signal, in pursuit of a predator, in chases of females by males or between rival

OPPOSITE Adults in summer
BELOW Adult in winter

males. But the outstanding aerial display is the male's 'tossing flight' (Hans Lind), called 'limping' by R. A. Richardson and W. F. Bishop, who describe graphically how he rises swiftly into an erratic orbit some 60 to 90 m. up, beating his wings, one half-flexed, one spread, at slightly different speeds, while the fanned tail is 'screwed' sideways and the bird calls grutto grutto (the Dutch name) for several minutes then suddenly 'arrows earthward' to land with his white-lined wings in a 'banner-like posture' and with a 'fanfare of whickering'. Lind distinguishes 5 phases in the flight and agrees that the wings move

differentially, something doubted by earlier
observers. The female may also 'sing' briefly and
pairs often fly together, calling or silent. The
male displays on the ground, fanning his tail at
a female or rival. The female stands still before
mating and the male flies up onto her from
behind, bending his legs as he grips her 'wrists'.

As with other waders, the male makes several ceremonial scrapes, the female eventually
choosing one. This is lined with grass and may
be well hidden, with a lattice of living stems over
it, or quite exposed, according to the habitat.
The clutch of 4 greenish to brown eggs, variably

marked with darker browns, is laid from the end
of March in the south and incubated by both
parents from the third or last egg. The downy
young, buffish above, white on cheeks and under
parts, hatch in 22 to 24 days and leave the nest on
an average 16 hours afterwards; they are looked
after by both parents and fly at about 4 weeks.
Black-tailed Godwits nest in loose colonies, frequently in association with other waders, especially Lapwings, which is interesting because both
are vigorous attackers of possible predators –
crows, hawks, big gulls and herons – the sitting
godwit often leaving the nest to join in the fray.

Limosa lapponica
BAR-TAILED GODWIT
SCOLOPACIDAE 36 to 38 cm. (including bill: 7·5 to 10 cm.)

The smaller and more northern of the 2 European godwits looks in winter like a small pale Curlew with its white V-shaped rump, greyish tail, lack of a wing-bar and dark primaries. Only at rest is it likely to be confused with its relative, though the shorter legs (in flight they barely project beyond the tail) and definitely uptilted bill are good characters. Also the under parts are whiter, while near at hand the upper parts are seen to be streaked and mottled. In summer plumage the male's under parts are much richer chestnut than those of the Black-tailed Godwit, almost mahogany (C. D. Minton) and the colour extends right to the under tail coverts. The female, larger and longer-billed than the male, is much paler, and brown streaks show up on her breast and flanks; in fact, juveniles show almost as much buff on their breasts, though in general they resemble dark-backed winter adults.

The European breeding status of the Bar-tailed Godwit depends on a small area in northern Scandinavia, extending eastwards through north-west Russia. The Asian range is a broader

some movement to the western parts of Britain and Ireland, and partly by way of the Black Sea to western Asia and north-east Africa; the Pacific race reaches Australia and New Zealand, and has not yet been recorded in Europe. Passage of the European and west Siberian breeding population is noted at Ottenby in southern Sweden at the end of July and during the first half of August; peak numbers in the Waddenzee (Netherlands) are reached in August. In late October enormous numbers (about 213,000 in 1973) assemble at the Banc d'Arguin in Mauretania. But a considerable wintering population remains in Britain and Ireland; over 54,000 birds were recorded in the estuaries count of January 1973 (A. J. Prater). These begin to leave in February and March for the Waddenzee, where they 'fatten up' for the breeding season, and are followed by the hordes from further south. But some thousands of probably immature birds, still in winter plumage, are present in April and May.

Rather more active than its larger relative, the Bar-tail walks quickly or runs along the shore, following the receding tide to take prey both from the surface and by thrusts into the mud, sometimes with a 'vigorous side-to-side movement of the head, much as a man moves his hand

OPPOSITE *Adult in summer*
BELOW *Adult in winter*

belt, largely above 70°N except where it approaches the Bering Strait, across which it continues into north-west Alaska and the Yukon Delta. East of Taimyr in Siberia birds are separated as the Pacific race *baueri*. In such northerly latitudes the typical habitat is swamp tundra or boggy country on the edge of the conifer taiga, where birds may perch on isolated trees.

But the Bar-tail becomes an inhabitant of sandy or muddy shores on passage and in winter, when its range overlaps that of the Black-tailed Godwit. The western population migrates partly through the Baltic and North Sea areas, with

in pushing a stick into the ground', to quote B. W. Tucker's apt simile. Crustaceans, small molluscs and marine worms are the main food with some small fish and, in summer, insects and their larvae and earthworms.

Bar-tailed Godwits often mix with other waders, but also form very large pure flocks, which are noted for their communal displays on the wing in winter. These become more dramatic as the spring migration approaches; the flock, which usually straggles or flies in wavy lines, comes together and then disintegrates as its members plunge downward, like 'whiffling'

geese, calling *kirric*, to sweep up again and repeat the wild descent. The *kirric* cry, less emphatic, is the usual call note; but this is a rather silent species except on the breeding grounds, where a variety of sounds has been described, including a 3-syllabled 'song', uttered in flight with alternate spells of fast flapping and gliding on stiff wings. The best known spring call, however, is a musical *weerka weerka*, resembling but distinct from the *whicka whicka* of the Black-tailed Godwit.

The usual nest site is on the open tundra, sometimes in very wet ground with scattered tussocks, but usually on a small hummock and lined with dead birch leaves, lichens or moss. The typical clutch is of 4 eggs, slightly glossy, olive or green with small spots and blotches of dark brown and ashy grey, sometimes very like eggs of the Black-tailed Godwit, but other types are more heavily marked. The male takes the greater share of the 3-week incubation. The downy chicks are more generally buff than young Black-tailed Godwits and are tended by both parents; they are said to fledge in about 3 weeks, and migration is soon under way from the breeding grounds.

Tringa ochropus
GREEN SANDPIPER
SCOLOPACIDAE 23 cm.

The smaller *Tringa* sandpipers are not prominent shore birds like their shorter-legged *Calidris* relatives, but they may be met with in the runnels of saltings and the tidal parts of small streams. This species, like the Storm Petrel, has been described as resembling a large House Martin and with rather more justice, as it not only has dark upper parts and a white rump, but its under parts are white both in winter and summer (shown on the plate). The 2 plumages are not readily separable in the field, but in winter the whitish spots on the back become buffish flecks and birds at rest can be confused with Wood Sandpipers. They always look darker and in flight the almost black underwing is quite distinctive; there is also much more white on the tail, which has only terminal black bars. The juvenile is scarcely to be told from the winter adult. The bill is blackish and the legs are olive green at all seasons.

The breeding range of the Green Sandpiper is an almost rectangular block of Eurasia from the Baltic and lower Danube across to the Pacific, mainly between 50° and 65°N. There are extensions into Norway, sporadically even to Scotland, and montane relict areas between the Black and Caspian seas and in Tien Shan. The habitat is forest land with plenty of bogs, pools, lakes and alder swamps. The western population breeds early and the moult begins in mid-June during migration. The wintering area is large and mainly inland, from Britain and the Netherlands to Iberia and countries bordering the Mediterranean, thence southward over much of Africa. Russian-ringed birds have been recovered in Tunisia. The eastern population winters from Sri Lanka to Indonesia.

The American equivalent of the Green Sandpiper is considered to be the Solitary Sandpiper, *T. solitaria* (a vagrant to Europe), and the adjective applies to this species as well, though often 2 birds are put up together. Larger parties may occur on passage but flocks are exceptional. 'Put up' expresses the usual situation: it is seldom that the observer sees the bird first, but it can sometimes be followed and watched at a distance when, like its relatives, it patters over the mud and constantly bobs its head and tail; it usually avoids standing right in the open. Feeding is by quick pecks at the ground or water, sometimes with deeper probing; the prey includes many insects and their larvae, spiders, small worms, crustaceans, and molluscs with some buds and shoots.

When flushed, the Green Sandpiper usually towers like a snipe, giving its attractive *tweet weet-weet* call, sometimes shortened to *too-eet* The song combines the usual breeding season note, a repeated *tit tit tit*, with the *too-eet*, as the male weaves circles in the air, now ascending with rapid beats, now gliding downwards. On the ground he lowers his head, droops his wings and raises the partly spread tail in display (D.

Nethersole-Thompson).

Although other waders do it, the Green Sandpiper is noted for its regular habit of occupying the old nests of a variety of birds from thrushes to crows and sometimes squirrels' dreys, adding practically no material but rearranging the old lining. The 4 eggs, laid from mid-April in the south, have a pale ground colour, from cream to light green, and are spotted and streaked with rich dark browns and purple-greys, often zoned at the larger end. Most of the 20 to 23 days incubation is performed by the female. The downy young are bright buff above with darker markings, and whitish below. After dropping from the nest, they move to a marsh or lakeside where they are first guided by both parents, later by the male alone. They fly at about 4 weeks old.

Tringa glareola
WOOD SANDPIPER
SCOLOPACIDAE 20 cm.

This species is even less of a shore haunter than the Green Sandpiper, but its habitat on passage is frequently coastal marshland and it may also be found in tidal creeks. In winter plumage it resembles its relative but has a greyish not blackish underwing and is generally less black and white in appearance; the rump but not so much of the tail is white. In summer the almost mottled upper parts are notable; at all times the pale superciliary stripes meet in a pronounced V above the bill. It also looks rather round headed and thin necked compared to its relatives. The juvenile has a buffish suffusion of the upper parts. The legs are more yellow than the Green Sandpiper's and project backward in flight to give a pointed tail effect.

The Wood Sandpiper's breeding range is more northerly and more extensive than the Green Sandpiper's, covering much of Eurasia from Scotland to Sakhalin between 50° and 70°N, with a small relict enclave in the Caucasus. The habitat includes forest, scrub and moorland with lakes and rivers, and the Finnish population alone has been estimated at 180,000 pairs. There is a well-defined migration to subtropical and tropical Africa, Asia and Australia. About 50,000 birds may pause to moult in the Camargue, but small flocks are usual on passage; wintering in Northern Europe is exceptional.

This is a more approachable bird than the Green Sandpiper but its habits are generally similar and it takes much the same types of food. The distinguishing call is *chiff chiff chiff* and 2 forms of song are used in display flights. The nest is usually fairly well hidden in grassy, or shrubby vegetation, but sometimes an old tree nest is taken. The 4 eggs are laid from late May and have a pale greenish ground with dark brown markings. Incubation is mainly by the female and lasts just over 3 weeks. The downy young resemble those of the Green Sandpiper and like them are tended first by both parents, later by the male only, flying in about 4 weeks.

Green Sandpiper in summer (below) and Wood Sandpiper (above)

Tringa hypoleucos
COMMON SANDPIPER
SCOLOPACIDAE 19·75 cm.

The smallest of the European *Tringa* sandpipers is often put in a separate genus *Actitis* on the rather slender grounds of its longish rounded tail and the nestling's distinctive plumage. The greyish-brown of the adult's upper parts extends right down the tail which, however, has white side feathers with dark bars; there is also a well-defined white wing-bar. In summer (as shown on the plate) the upper parts are lightly barred and flecked with dark brown; in winter they are more nearly uniform. Apart from a variable amount of brown streaking on the neck and upper breast, the under parts are white in both plumages. Juveniles show barring on the upper parts due to the buffish margins of the feathers, which are otherwise rather darker than on adults.

If, as suggested by K. H. Voous and others, the American Spotted Sandpiper, *T. macularia*, is regarded as a race of this species, its breeding distribution covers most of the northern hemisphere above 30°N and below 65°N; there is also a remarkable enclave in the mountains of Kenya and Uganda. The Common Sandpiper breeds in all the countries of Northern Europe, very commonly in some, but is rare in Belgium, the Netherlands and Denmark which lack its favoured habitats: high level bare or wood-fringed lakes, streams and rivers (up to 3000 m. in Switzerland) and sheltered but rocky inlets of the sea. Hardly has passage northward eased off in June before the return movement, perhaps headed by failed breeders, begins and continues well into the autumn, usually in small parties along the coast or inland. The wintering area is enormous, odd birds remaining in or near the breeding range, while the majority spread throughout the subtropics and tropics and beyond, to Australia including Tasmania, South Africa and northern Argentina.

In human terms the Common Sandpiper is an excitable bird; on the ground it continually bobs its head and tail up and down independently, then takes off into the unique flight used over short distances, the bowed wings moving jerkily like an oarsman's sculls; then it glides to land again with fluttering wings. This is accompanied either by the *twee wee-wee* call, the emphasis on the first syllable, or, in spring, by the *kittywiper* 'song', also uttered from the ground or a perch. Parties flying long distances have a more normal beating flight like other waders. When feeding, birds may progress quite silently, pecking worms and snails out of the mud, snapping up flying insects, or wading into shallow water after crustaceans. Feeding is usually solitary, but flocks may form for roosting, probably as a prelude to migration (J. L. F. Parslow).

Much of the display takes place in the air, the male chanting his *kittywipers* as he circles over prospective territory or mate. Both sexes may fly together on an erratic course or male may chase female ceremonially, with slow wing-beats. At times several males may be in the air together. The male displays on the ground, running with one or both wings raised, sometimes chasing the female. He also defends her against other males and a pair will attack much larger predators boldly, uttering a loud version of the *twee wee-wee* call.

The nest sites chosen by Common Sandpipers are extremely varied; though not recorded from an old tree nest like its larger relatives, it has used the nest of a Ring Ousel, *Turdus torquatus*, in a bank and has laid in a pollard willow. Nests on the ground may be in woods or on open moorland, be well hidden in thick vegetation or quite exposed on river shingle, but the majority are probably on a bank of some kind. Some consist of a substantial pad of dead plant material, others have only a fine lining. The slightly glossy eggs are, for a wader, fairly uniform, with a pinkish cream ground and small dark chestnut spots often concentrated at the larger end; sometimes there are relatively few larger blotches; there are ashy 'background' spots as well. The usual clutch is 4, laid from the second half of April in the south, and their incubation, by both sexes, lasts about 3 weeks. The upper parts of the chicks appear rather uniform greyish brown, due to the black tips of the buff down; there are several black stripes, including one through the eye; the under parts are mainly white. Both parents guard the brood, one signalling to the other the approach of danger and setting up a chorus of alarm calls. The young fly when about 4 weeks old.

Injury-feigning is regular and has been seen from a pair at an empty nest scrape, both fanning tails and one flopping away through the vegetation. These birds had been giving the *kittywiper* cry, but a bird coming off eggs with spread tail and quivering wings gave 2 loud shrieks in addition. Individuals vary in their behaviour and many slip off the nest and fly away quietly.

The Spotted Sandpiper, mentioned above, is a vagrant to Northern Europe. The primarily Asian Terek Sandpiper, *Xenus cinereus* (sometimes called *T. terek*), nests in northern and central European Russia and, very locally, in Finland. It is about 23 cm. long, grey-brown above with converging dark stripes on the back, and white below with some streaking at the side of the neck. The long yellow to grey bill is decidedly uptilted; the yellow legs are rather short. Coastal islands (in the Gulf of Bothnia) are included in the breeding habitat; on passage and in winter it is found in South-east Asia, Australia and South Africa, on low-lying shores and estuaries.

Adult in summer

Tringa totanus
REDSHANK
SCOLOPACIDAE 28 cm.

This is one of the best-known medium-sized waders of temperate Eurasia, partly because it is one of the noisiest, putting marsh or shore on the alert with its musical but penetrating alarm call and therefore equally unwelcome to wildfowler and bird-watcher. At a distance the Redshank's upper parts, including the breast, appear uniform grey-brown in all plumages; then the bird takes off to reveal a broad white bar on the secondaries, a V-shaped white rump, whitish underwings and a grey-barred tail beyond which the orange-yellow legs project slightly. The winter plumage is shown on the plate; in summer the upper parts are browner, with overlying blackish streaks; the primaries are always blackish brown. The juvenile is like a heavily marked summer adult, with paler legs. The bill is pink at the base, dark at the tip.

The breeding range extends across Eurasia roughly on either side of 50°N and includes Iceland, the Faeroe Islands, Britain and Ireland. But the Redshank is now very local elsewhere in western Europe. Further east it reaches south to the Caucasus and as far as 30°N in Tibet and China. The favoured summer habitat is grassland or heath, often damp, sometimes quite dry and elevated but extending to saltings, sand dunes and shingle beaches with very light vegetation. Wooded country, except very open scrub in the north, is avoided. Several races have been separated, of which the Icelandic *robusta* is partly resident, partly migratory to western Europe and North Africa. The British and Irish *britannica* deserts its inland breeding grounds but may only move down to the coast, whereas continental birds reach South Africa and the Asian population winters in Indonesia and the Philippines. At this season Redshanks are birds principally of estuary and muddy shore, but some frequent rocky coasts with Turnstones. At the peak of passage in September 1972 the British and Irish estuarine population was over 113,000 birds.

Usually appearing restless, even agitated, the Redshank is often on the move, investigating the mud with its bill, crossing shallow inlets by wading or swimming, then pausing to bob, first head up, then tail up, before giving the single *tew* or triple *tew hew hew* call and rising into its strong but jerky flight. The varied diet of small invertebrates is taken from vegetation, snapped up in shallow water or extracted from the ground by probing 5 cm. deep. On a north-east Scottish estuary a Redshank has been estimated to take some 40,000 prey a day at a rate of one per second. In winter it feeds into the night, sifting the mud through its open mandibles; it also takes earthworms and leather jackets from the fields. When feeding between the tide lines birds may operate singly, with other waders, or in small parties. The large flocks are seen on passage or when resting at high tide.

Master of an extensive vocabulary, the Red-shank has several explosive alarm calls besides the *tew hew hew* and the monotonous *chip chip chip*, frequently uttered from a post or other high perch by birds with young at risk. Two calls often given in flight may be regarded as songs: a single, repeated *tut tut tut*, particularly associated with display, and a double note used, as most of the calls are, by both sexes. Display may begin communally among the flocks, but males arrive first on the breeding grounds. When they have attracted a mate, both fly together over their territory. In the song flight the bird rises 'with rapid, shivering wing-action' (B. W. Tucker) before setting its wings as it approaches its zenith, then sinking or gliding downwards. On the ground the male pursues the female with fanned tail, finally approaching her from behind with a flutter of raised wings, their white undersides visible at a distance, to mount and mate.

Although usually quite well hidden, Redshanks' nests may be exposed when on sand or shingle. A common choice is beside a tuft of vegetation or in a patch rather higher than the surrounding level. In thick grass the blades are often twined together overhead, evidently by the female, who lines the scrape with dry stems. The canopy, which gives the site away to a human observer, must have survival value against other predators or the weather. Laying may begin early in April in the south of the range; the usual clutch is 4, though it is not unknown for more than one female to lay in a nest. The eggs are less variable than those of many waders, rather like large Common Sandpipers' eggs with a creamy to buff ground and fairly small reddish-brown spots concentrated at the large end; sometimes the marking is heavier, almost blotched. Both parents incubate the eggs, which hatch in 23–24 days. The downy chicks are buff-brown above with a pattern of blackish streaks, and have white underparts. At first both parents look after them, later the male only; they fly in about 4 weeks and soon leave the nesting area.

Redshanks usually slip off the nest quietly long before an intruder draws near and there is often a close association with breeding groups of Lapwings, nests of the 2 species being sometimes only a metre or so apart. As Lapwings lay earlier and therefore become demonstrative earlier, when their eggs are near hatching they must provide some protective cover. Redshanks at the same stage may sit tight, shrieking at the intruder if disturbed.

The Spotted or Dusky Redshank, *Tringa erythropus*, is slightly larger (about 30 cm. long) yet more elegant than its commoner relative, being longer-billed and longer-legged. In summer it is black with white spots on the back; in winter it is greyish, but can at all times be distinguished from the Redshank by its lack of a wing-bar and distinctive *tchoo-it* flight call. It breeds from northern Scandinavia east across Eurasia between 65° and 75°N and winters in the Mediterranean area, Africa and southern Asia, being seen on passage both inland and on estuaries, where the British population in October 1972 was 485 birds.

A group in winter

Tringa nebularia
GREENSHANK
SCOLOPACIDAE 30 cm.

Formerly the egg-collector's most teasing quarry, the Greenshank is one of the largest of the *Tringa* waders, a generally scarce and solitary bird. Its Finnish breeding population has been estimated at 30,000 pairs, but the peak total on British and Irish estuaries during passage in September 1972 was around 1300 birds. About the same size as a Spotted Redshank, the Greenshank looks definitely bulkier than the common Redshank and can be distinguished at a reasonable distance from either species by its greyish-green leg colour and by the slightly uptilted bill; from the Spotted Redshank also by its lighter head and neck in summer; from the Redshank by the all-dark wing and apparently white tail in flight. The summer plumage is shown on the plate; in winter the Greenshank appears greyish-white at a distance, darker on a closer view: the feathers of the upper parts have white margins, etched on the inner sides with black. Like Redshanks, juvenile Greenshanks resemble rather dark summer adults, but are more evenly patterned.

Somewhat more northerly than the Redshank, the Greenshank breeds across Eurasia from the Scottish Highlands and north-western Scandinavia to Sakhalin on the Pacific, broadly between 55° and 65°N, though extending beyond 70°N in Norway. The habitat ranges from bare tundra and moorland to open conifer and birch forest, with bogs, pools and larger waters as the common denominator. The Greenshank is replaced in the muskegs of North America by the very similar Greater Yellowlegs, *T. melanoleuca*. After nesting, the birds leave their usually rather barren breeding grounds for lowland waters and riversides, the majority in the west reaching estuaries and sheltered shores, occasionally quite rocky ones. One migration route is southwest from the Baltic to the Atlantic coast of Europe; another is overland to Greece and thence probably across the Sahara to the Niger inundation zone in West Africa. While small numbers winter not far from their breeding area, others cross the tropics to South Africa, Sri Lanka, Indonesia and Australasia.

A ringing *tew tew tew* call is the usual announcement of the Greenshank's presence, preceding the sight of a single bird or small party, twisting in flight, then straightening out to land with a run almost on the edge of the water, the white rump area catching the eye before the dark wings close over it. Perching above ground level is rare outside the breeding season, when trees, posts and prominent boulders are freely used. The Greenshank's feeding habits comprise an Avocet-like side to side movement of the bill along the surface of the water as well as direct pecking and probing. Small fish are pursued in the shallows with neck stretched and bill held underwater, 'as if pushing a lawnmower' (S. Dillon Ripley and Salim Ali). But the main food is invertebrate: insects and their larvae, small crustaceans and molluscs, and worms. Tadpoles as well as fish up to 7·5 cm. long are caught. Greenshanks may often be found up the quiet creeks frequented by redshanks and Green Sandpipers. A flock of over 50 seems to be exceptional anywhere.

The triple *tew*, sometimes followed by *tewi tewi tewi*, is only the best known of a large repertoire of calls, which have been studied by D. Nethersole-Thompson. He has shown that calls and displays may occur in several different contexts during the breeding season, when 'the most significant call is the quickly repeated and incessant *chipping*', (also rendered *tchook*). This is used by both sexes during courtship and mating, from their arrival on the breeding grounds in late March or early April until they leave. It has been particularly associated with the twice-daily change-over at the nest. The song is a 'rich modulated *too-hoo*', uttered in 'sustained bursts' in the display flight but varying, according to Nethersole-Thompson, with the emotional state of the bird. The male arrives first at the nesting area and begins 'advertising' for a mate and proclaiming territorial ownership. Re-mating with the same bird is quite usual and pairs may persist for several years. Confusingly, joint song flights may be made by the pair or by rival males; 'the two birds rise . . . with strong clipping wing-beats, and the tortuous low-flying sex chase often occurs before pursuer and chased rise high to career madly, turning and swerving together'. A mile or more may be covered before the flight ends in 'a spectacular dive or zoom earthwards'. The mating routine resembles that of the Redshank, 'with ecstatic wing-shivering' by the male before and while he mounts the female on the ground. Mating may also take place on trees, rocks, fences and even be attempted in the air.

Unlike some other waders, the female Greenshank does the preliminary nest-scraping, though the male may 'suggest' likely spots. Nests are predominantly close to a rock, fallen timber or tree stump, but sometimes by a mossy hummock and are lined with local materials. Laying begins in the south of the range before the end of April and the 4 eggs appear at 36 or 48 hour intervals. They are like large Redshank's eggs but usually with the markings well distributed over the surface. Both parents incubate them and the changes-over, early in the morning and in the evening, give the best opportunity of tracking this tight-sitting bird to its nest in featureless moorland. The eggs hatch in 24 to 25 days and, as the day approaches, the parents' behaviour changes and they mob intruders violently. The downy chicks, patterned like baby Redshanks, but darker brown above and greyish-white below, are soon taken to the shores of a loch or pool when they learn to feed, the parents continuing their strident defence until the young fly in just under 4 weeks.

Adult in summer

Calidris canutus
KNOT
SCOLOPACIDAE 25 cm.

The specific name was bestowed by Linnaeus, apparently following a suggestion by Camden that it was a visitor to Britain from Denmark. More colourful is the view that, by daring the tide's advance, the Knot resembled the Danish king, and called his name *Knut* at the same time. In fact, the plump and stocky Knot is the largest and one of the most numerous members of its genus in Northern Europe in winter. All the same, although the biggest Dunlins are not more than 19 cm. long, flocks of the 2 species at a distance may be difficult to tell apart without any standard of comparison. Winter Knots are, however, paler than Dunlins but not so white as Sanderlings. Close at hand the straight, relatively short black bill is distinctive and in flight the Knot shows blackish primaries, a not very pronounced white wing-bar and, more obviously, an almost white rump and tail, whereas Dunlin and Sanderling have uniformly darker rumps and tails, with white at the sides. The Knot's under parts are white, with grey on the neck and barred flanks. There is a striking transformation in spring: head and under parts become rich chestnut, the back is mottled black and chestnut and the crown streaked black; the wings remain much as in winter. The juvenile has buffish under parts; its upper parts look scaly, due to narrow black and white borders to the feathers of the back.

Like the Grey Plover, the Knot is a high arctic species, breeding only marginally and perhaps not regularly in Northern Europe, in part of Svalbard. The typical race *canutus* nests in the Taimyr Peninsula of Asian Siberia, and in the New Siberian and Wrangel Islands, while the race *rufa* breeds very locally in northern Alaska and in scattered localities in the coasts of arctic Canada and Greenland. K. H. Voous believes that this curious distribution is partly due to the scarcity of the preferred habitat, stony lichen-covered tundra, and partly to the vicissitudes of the species in the ice ages. The Knot spends not much more than 2 months on its inhospitable breeding grounds and then begins its long migration south again. Concentrated ringing has shown that birds from Greenland pass through or winter in Britain, and a British ring from a Knot was found in the pellet of a Gyrfalcon, *Falco rusticolus*, on Ellesmere Island in the Canadian arctic. A bird ringed in Norfolk in March 1971 was found in Barbados the following August, perhaps suggesting an intended change of winter quarters. Another, August-ringed, Knot from Norfolk was reported the following July near Gdańsk (Danzig) on the Polish Baltic shore, indicating a Siberian breeding area. The speed record goes to a juvenile, ringed in Norfolk in September and recovered 8 days later 6440 km. away in Liberia. But though

Knots go far south, to Patagonia, South Africa and Australasia, as far as Macquarie Island (about 55°S), it is likely that the majority of the world population winters in Britain and Ireland, where the 1972-3 counts gave peaks approaching 300,000 birds. An estimate for the continental coasts of north-western Europe is about 130,000 birds. Non-breeding one-year-olds also spend the summer in Britain, sometimes showing good plumage, but moulting towards the end of May, some 2 months ahead of the main period.

Knots may pack so close in their favoured estuaries that they look from afar like another kind of grey mud. These phalanxes have been captured by photographers at places like Hilbre in the Welsh Dee Estuary, waiting for the tide to turn and allow them to spread out in search of the small molluscs and crustaceans for which they probe as they run busily over the flats. They also fly in close order, performing the classic now dark, now light manoeuvres as the wheeling movement ripples through a great flock. The usual calls at this time are the single *knut* and the higher-pitched *wit-wit*. Knots mix freely with other waders on the shore and some may join Turnstones and Purple Sandpipers on rocky stretches; but inland occurrences are few, probably of birds interrupting a cross-country flight.

A full account of breeding Knots comes from D. N. Nettleship's study of them on Ellesmere Island, where they arrive by way of Iceland in late May and early June; the sexes are together and soon pairs are covering the snow-free areas at a density of about one to the square km., gathering in small flocks to feed. At first their diet is the reproductive parts of the sparse vegetation: sedges, mare's-tails, *Polygonum* species and mosses, with a change about mid-June to insect larvae, mainly chironomid midges. These appear as adults by the time the young Knots are hatched, more or less synchronously, to take advantage of this brief plenitude of prey.

The Knot's most striking display is the male's song flight. After rising steeply anything from 20 to 160 m. above ground, he first glides with wings held diagonally upwards, calling a repeated *whip poo mee*; in the second phase the wings are held horizontal and the 'song' shortened to *poo mee*; finally there is a rapid flapping action and calls every second before the final glide to earth. Each phase lasts 5 to 10 seconds and a series of flights for 5 to 10 minutes. Mating on the ground is accompanied by wailing cries.

The exposed nest scrapes are lined with lichens, and the 4 eggs laid from early June, pale green in ground with a variety of well scattered markings. Both sexes incubate them, and the downy young, mottled buff and blackish above with white spots, and white below, hatch in about 22 days. The male does most of the tending, soon leading them to rich feeding areas. They fledge in about 3 weeks, then gather into small flocks before migration.

*Summer adult (bottom), in transitional plumage
(centre left), immature bird (centre right) and winter
adult (top)*

Calidris maritima
PURPLE SANDPIPER
SCOLOPACIDAE 20 cm.

Although not as familiar as the Dunlin, Ringed Plover or Common Sandpiper, this is the most confiding of the smaller shore waders, and its liking for maritime artefacts – piers, harbour walls, breakwaters – means that it can often be watched close to scenes of busy human activity.

Its dark and dumpy form with legs of variable but prominent shades of yellow, together with its preference for rocky or stony shores, makes the Purple Sandpiper easy to identify in winter. The purplish gloss, masked in summer by the rufous margins of the back feathers, is also most in evidence then. But the general impression is of grey-brown above, shading to the white under parts. The very pale underwing and a white bar on the secondaries show in flight; the rump and white-edged tail have a black central line.

Juveniles superficially resemble adults but many wing feathers and the upper tail coverts have creamy tips which, though worn, persist into the first summer plumage. The upper parts of the downy nestling are a variegated 'velvety-brown and yellowish-buff' (H. F. Witherby), effectively cryptic in the breeding habitat.

Purple Sandpipers and Turnstones are typical associates on passage and in winter on rocky coasts but the larger bird is not always a guide to the smaller which, partly because of its indifference to man and immobility, may be quite difficult to spot only a few yards away. Then the party, usually not more than a dozen or so but occasionally as many as 100, suddenly takes wing with quiet *wit-wit* calls and curves over the water to a new perch, almost vanishing against the dark weed-grown rocks.

The breeding range is circumpolar but extremely fragmented, lying between 60° and 80°N (the range of the closely related, possibly conspecific Rock Sandpiper, *C. ptilocnemis*, of Alaska and the Bering coasts extends further south) through arctic Canada, Greenland, Iceland, northern Scandinavia and the arctic archipelagos to Taimyr and New Siberian Islands, the habitat being either tundra or the alpine zone up to 500 m.; there has been some contraction northward in recent years. Malcolm Ogilvie has described the Purple Sandpiper as 'probably the most northerly wintering wader in the world', remaining in parts of the breeding range where the seas are ice-free and seldom coming south of 45°N in its autumn migration.

At this period and in winter the main food is small crustaceans and molluscs, deftly captured from rock crevices and under seaweed as the tide ebbs, the birds sometimes wading and even swimming as they hunt. A recent study by C. J. Feare in north-east England showed that winkles, dog whelks, mussels and shore crabs were the principal prey. Sometimes they forage inland, even, according to Esther Waters, among the Grey Seals of North Rona (North Scotland). Small fish (gobies) and fish eggs are other items recorded.

In summer on the breeding grounds the preferred food becomes insects but, if these are scarce, Purple Sandpipers turn vegetarian and O. Le Roi found only buds, leaves, and the remains of algae, mosses and diatoms in 18 out of 25 stomachs examined. Otherwise a variety of insects, especially springtails and, from fresh water, chironomid flies are taken, with some arachnids and annelid worms.

On the breeding ground the Purple Sandpiper becomes vocal and many notes have been described. Ogilvie, who has recently studied the bird in Svalbard, distinguishes a high-pitched trill of alarm, a wheezy call on a slightly descending scale, used in display, and 'a rather complicated song . . . essentially a series of short notes, each repeated three or four times'. The display flight is 'invariably accompanied by the song' and is primarily territorial. The male climbs about 30 m., then describes wide circles before gliding swiftly to earth with wings held above his back. He may also fly with 'slow, abrupt wing-beats' or glide in circles, uttering the wheezy call; sometimes he flies with wings quivering and held low.

Exposure of the whitish underwing is also a feature of ground displays, one or both wings being raised and lowered quickly. This 'wing-lift' is used when courting, as an aggressive display, and when alarmed, even by tiny chicks (P. O. Swanberg). Ogilvie also noted that alarmed birds may stand erect with necks stretched or crouch and even run with legs bent. The crouching posture is also used in courtship chases, but the 'fast erratic flights' are more spectacular and end with the male overhauling and gliding in front of the female, his wings held stiff as he gives the display call.

The nest of the Purple Sandpiper is one of the hardest to find of all waders. In Svalbard Ogilvie found broods up to 400 m. apart, which leaves a great deal of featureless tundra to be searched. Somewhere in this the male scrapes 2 or more nest cups, one of which his mate chooses. An 'active' cup (preserved by the snow, scrapes may persist over winter) is lined with tiny leaves and receives 4, sometimes 3 pear-shaped eggs, with a green ground when fresh and heavily marked and spotted with rich brown. They are laid from early June onwards and hatch in about 3 weeks. The male does most of the incubation (though the female has brood-patches too) and raises the brood on his own, like several other waders.

The Purple Sandpiper usually sits very closely and, when flushed, performs the classic 'rodent run' distraction display, fluttering away over the ground, wings trailing to look like hind-legs, and tail spread, the central dark line simulating a rodent's tail. S-A. Bengtson followed one displaying bird for 1200 m.

Adult in summer

Calidris minuta
LITTLE STINT
SCOLOPACIDAE 14 to 15 cm.

About half the size of a Knot, this is probably the best known in Northern Europe of the little *Calidris* sandpipers. These minuscule waders include a number of puzzling vagrants from North America. The Little Stint is smaller than the smallest Dunlin, looking in winter grey above and white below, but with a short straight bill, whereas the Dunlin's is relatively longer and slightly curved. The plumage most often seen is that of the first autumn, when the upper parts are mottled buff and black, with a noticeable pale V pointing tailwards. The under parts are washed buff; the cheeks, forehead and pronounced superciliary stripe are whitish. The summer plumage is altogether richer, almost rufous above and on the breast and cheeks, with some darker mottling. As the feathers wear, both adults and juveniles appear darker. The primaries are black, there is a narrow white wing-bar and the rump and tail are centrally dark as on the Dunlin, with white showing on the edge of the tail coverts. The legs are black.

The Little Stint has a restricted breeding range from about 30° to 130°E along the northern coasts of Eurasia, mainly in the littoral and valley zones of the moss tundra. But birds on passage pass along the shores and appear inland throughout Europe, on their way to winter from the Camargue to South Africa and in southern

season, with some plant seeds. Flocks of Little Stints perform aerial evolutions like their relatives. The usual call or alarm note is a reiterated *chit*, which becomes a continuous low twitter when the flock is feeding. A number of other calls are associated with passage, including a shortened version of the song in spring. This trilling or buzzing may be heard on the ground or accompanying the hovering display flight.

Most Little Stints nest on the edge of marshy tundra but sometimes at some altitude inland. The site, which may be sheltered by low scrub, is a shallow scrape lined with leaves and stems. The clutch of 4 eggs, pale olive to buff with rich dark brown and 'underlying' grey speckles and blotches, is laid from mid-June and incubated mainly by the male. Injury-feigning off the nest or when young are about is common. The male probably has the major role in tending the chicks, which are warm buff mottled black, above, with white foreheads and under parts. Their fledging period is undetermined, but they flock on the breeding ground before migrating.

Calidris temminckii
TEMMINCK'S STINT
SCOLOPACIDAE 14 cm.

This is far less of a shore bird than the Little Stint, but may be found in tidal creeks and runnels in the saltings, towering up to plump down again quickly. More uniformly grey than the Little Stint in all plumages, Temminck's Stint

OPPOSITE *Little Stints in winter, adults (left)
and juvenile (right)*
BELOW *Temminck's Stints in summer*

Asia. Few winter as far north as Britain.

Several *Calidris* species are noted for their tameness with man and the Little Stint can often be closely approached as it runs about the muddy shore, pecking quickly at the surface. According to B. A. Bengtsson's and B. Svensson's study in south Sweden, insects hunted by sight are the main prey. Whereas on the coast it frequently mixes with the related Dunlin and Curlew Sandpiper, on East African lakes it associates on the lily pads with *Tringa* species like Common and Wood Sandpipers. Insects are certainly its major food during the breeding

has a greyish rather than white breast. In summer (as shown) the upper parts are grey-brown with rufous margins to the blackish feathers; this mottled effect is lost in autumn. The juveniles at close range look scaly, due to pale feather margins. The wing pattern is like that of the Little Stint, but the outer tail feathers are white; the legs vary from yellow to brown.

Temminck's Stint has a more extensive and rather more southerly breeding range than the Little Stint, nesting sporadically, perhaps now regularly, in Britain, locally in southern Norway, more generally in northern Scandinavia whence

the distribution runs east on either side of 70°N to the Pacific. The favoured habitats are shrub tundra, the birch zone, grassy fields and riverine islands, to heaths at 1000 m. Passage is mainly inland, with stops by rivers and pools, to wintering areas in Africa and southern Asia.

Usually solitary or in small parties, flocks of Temminck's Stint form in autumn, when they are seen on the Baltic coasts, and mix with other species. They feed like Little Stints by pecking rather than probing, taking mainly insects and their larvae and earthworms. The usual call is a 'high-pitched trilling titter' (B. W. Tucker) and

the song, given in moth-like 'yo-yo' flight, is a trill sustained for a minute or more; it is also uttered on the ground accompanied by wing-flicking. The displays are stimulated by other males in the breeding group.

The nest is usually near water, sometimes exposed, or hidden in low scrub. The 3 to 4 eggs resemble the Little Stint's and are laid from mid-June. This is one of the waders which quite often lays 2 clutches, each parent incubating one (O. Hildén). The downy chicks, paler than Little Stints, hatch in about 3 weeks and fledge in 2 to $2\frac{1}{2}$ weeks, tended by one or both parents.

Calidris alpina

DUNLIN

SCOLOPACIDAE 17 to 19 cm.

This is the most numerous small wader of the North European shores on passage or in winter, when its population in British and Irish estuaries may exceed half a million. It is predominantly a grey bird with black legs and a variable, often slightly curved bill, longer on average in the female than the male. Actually the upper parts are greyish-brown, streaked with black, as is the breast. In summer there is a striking change to richer colours above, while the irregular black patch on the lower breast is distinctive. Juveniles in autumn resemble adults, but have paler feather margins on the back, rather dull buff breasts and streaks or spots on their flanks. Various stages of plumage may be seen in the same flock. On the wing the flight feathers and the central rump and tail look blackish, with a narrow white wing-bar and white edges to the tail.

The Dunlin has a discontinuous circumpolar breeding range. K. H. Voous believes that the southern breeding population in Britain, Ireland and round the Baltic is a relic of an earlier post-glacial distribution. But via northern Scandinavia it is connected with the populations along the arctic coasts of Eurasia to Alaska, while, via the Faeroe Islands, and Iceland where it is common, it is linked with populations in Greenland and arctic Canada. The habitat therefore varies from tundra of several types and arctic-alpine moorland to lush bogs and even salt marshes with short, tufty vegetation. The more northerly and the barren inland breeding areas are left in autumn and there is a general movement south, the northern race *alpina* replacing the southern *schinzii* in the British area. But wintering Dunlins are not common south of 25°N. Intensive ringing has shown that, as well as birds from northern Scandinavia and Russia, Dunlins from Iceland and Greenland visit Britain on passage or in winter, while birds ringed in autumn in Britain have been recovered in Mauretania, one after only 17 days in September 1972. In spring a bird ringed in Cheshire was recovered in Greenland 15 days later.

Huge flocks of Dunlin are traditional; hence it may be puzzling when single birds occur, inland or on the coast. On their favourite muddy or sandy shores they associate with many other species, especially with Ringed Plovers, though their feeding methods are quite different. Superficially Dunlins appear to move quickly over the shore, pecking and probing. Sometimes a bird may catch sight of movement and snatch its prey after a quick dash. More often it 'sounds' the mud and, if encouraged by this, probes with mandibles slightly apart, finally going down as much as 1·5 cm. to seize a worm, enclosing it between the mandibles in a series of thrusts (J. M. Dewar). Dunlins may also patter with their feet on the surface like other waders and gulls, apparently to attract worms upwards. The ragworm, *Nereis diversicolor*, is a favourite prey in south Sweden; small molluscs and crustaceans are also taken and, in summer, the larvae of tipulid and chironomid flies as well as adult insects. As the tide flows, the Dunlins bunch and retreat, sometimes taking wing and indulging in the concerted aerobatics for which wader flocks are famous. Then they land with a flutter of wings and sink into repose, bills housed on their backs, often standing on one leg, until the ebb summons them to feed again.

Flocks on the wing do not usually call very much, but small parties and single birds emit the shrill reel which is a characteristic estuarine sound, and is used also in the breeding season, forming the basis of the full, rippling trill which the male utters on his hovering lark-like display flight, up to 75 m. high, over his territory. Several birds may also chase wildly on the wing and there is a ground display, with flashing of the white underwings. The female trills from the ground; often she and her mate occupy slight eminences, peat hummocks, boulders, and reel at the intruder on the breeding ground, interspersing this with a rather deep *quot quot*.

Dunlins often nest in loose groups, surviving males returning to the same sites. The nest is in a grass tuft, among heather or other low shrubs, frequently on the edge of a wet patch, and is lined with stems or leaves. The 4 eggs, laid at 1½-day intervals from late April, vary from green or blue-green to buff and brown, finely or thickly spotted and streaked in a characteristic spiral twist with dark and red browns and underlying grey. The male takes an increasing share of the incubation and the female sometimes disappears before the hatch after about 3 weeks. On average she leaves 6 days after it (M. Soikkeli in south Finland) and the male too may desert the brood before they fledge at 20 days old. At first the young are downy, black, buff and richer brown above, whitish below, and feed largely on small chironomid flies (R. T. Holmes in Alaska). Although the Dunlin, like most other waders, is single-brooded, Soikkeli found 3 females who remated with fresh males and laid second clutches, leaving their original mates with the first broods.

In winter plumage (above and below), in summer
(centre left) and in transitional plumage (centre right)

Calidris ferruginea
CURLEW SANDPIPER
SCOLOPACIDAE   19 cm.

This is very much a bird-watcher's bird, closely resembling the Dunlin with which it commonly associates on passage, but clearly distinguished in flight by its white rump and blackish tail. When these cannot be seen, the curved bill which leads to the first part of its name is not altogether reliable, since many Dunlins have bills as much or even more curved at the tip. But the Curlew Sandpiper is a relatively taller, longer-legged, longer-necked, smaller-headed bird, with more pronounced pale superciliary and dark eye stripes. Juvenile birds, which predominate on autumn passage, look smoothly scaly above, an effect due to the light buff margins of the dark back feathers. The white under parts shade to a pale russet throat, giving the bird a somewhat 'cleaner' look than a Dunlin. The adult's grey winter plumage is very much like the Dunlin's with its white under parts, but in spring these become a rich chestnut, like the Knot's and the godwits', while the back acquires a black mottling, adding to the bird's striking appearance. The female is somewhat duller than the male. The wing pattern in all plumages is virtually the same as the Dunlin's.

In Northern Europe the Curlew Sandpiper is only seen on passage, as its breeding range is confined to arctic Siberia eastward from the Gyda Peninsula and mouth of the Yenisei River to the New Siberian Islands and the Kolyma Delta. In 1962 breeding was attempted near Barrow, Alaska. The favourite habitat is on the drier south-facing slopes of the tundra above a river valley. There appear to be 2 main passage routes, a northerly one by way of the Baltic coasts, the North Sea and the British area, and a southerly one which crosses the Black Sea and Asia Minor. But a juvenile ringed in Lincolnshire in September 1969 was shot in the Crimea in August 1972, suggesting that the same route may not be used each year. On British and Irish estuaries August is the peak month of passage with 404 birds reported in 1972, as against some 125,000 Dunlins, an indication of the species' relative scarcity, though numbers fluctuate annually and may in some years, as in 1969, reach thousands. Spring passage through Britain is much lighter than in autumn and only occasional birds spend the winter so far north. The main areas are from the Mediterranean south to South Africa and from southern Asia to Australia, Tasmania and New Zealand, where the birds stay from September until April. Some non-breeders may remain through the northern summer.

On passage Curlew Sandpipers are seen singly, in small parties, sometimes in flocks of hundreds. Their habits are similar to those of the Dunlin, though they perhaps move more quickly and cover longer distances between feeding points. Their prey and methods of obtaining it appear to be generally similar; but as well as molluscs and crustaceans on the shore they take insects and their larvae: Neuroptera, beetles and flies, feeding a little way inland in tall grassland. Feeding flocks twitter quietly and this is probably the same note as the *tirri tirri* of wintering birds; the usual call at all seasons is a quiet chirrup. The alarm note on the breeding grounds, *wiek wiek wiek*, was described by Miss M. D. Haviland who, equally competent with camera or collector's gun, visited arctic Siberia just before the First World War.

R. T. Holmes and F. A. Pitelka, studying the attempted breeding in Alaska, recognized these calls and many others, including a sharp *chit* and the whine, 'a clear melodic ascending *whaay whaay*' which can be heard hundreds of metres away. It is a component of the elaborate song, delivered in flight and lasting 10 to 15 seconds, with introductory notes, a series of 'trilled doublets', a complex 4-part phrase and the final whine. Males chase females in the air, sometimes gliding after them, and patrol their considerable territories with a special slow-beating flight. On the ground intruders of other species are attacked at a run, with tail lowered and spread.

Nest-scraping and grass-tossing over the shoulder, accompanied by elements of the song, may attract the female to the rudimentary cup, but this seems unlikely to be the one she chooses to lay in eventually. Finally, there is the pre-mating display, in which the male raises his wings, that nearer the female first, stretches his neck, uttering the 'trilled doublets', and lowers and fans the tail with his back to the female, exposing the white rump. The female dashes at it, then walks away, at which the male follows and mounts her.

The same tundra area may be used by small groups of Curlew Sandpipers in successive years, the old nest scrapes being preserved in the hard ground: they are usually situated on low hummocks of moss and sparse vegetation and scantily lined. The normal clutch is 4 and eggs are laid from mid-summer onwards. They are matt-surfaced and show a variable greenish ground with bold dark and reddish brown spots and blotches and purple underlying marks. Incubation, as far as is known, is by the female only; after hatching she leads the downy chicks, which resemble pale baby Dunlins, off the slopes to boggy ground. The whole cycle, from first egg to fledging, lasts about 6 weeks.

Holmes and Pitelka considered that the complex displays of the Curlew Sandpiper were allied to those of the Pectoral Sandpiper, *C. melanotos*, the American wader most frequently recorded in Northern Europe, nearly always in autumn. It is 18 to 20 cm. long, the upper parts streaked blackish, brown and buff, with a clearly defined edge between the breast and the white under parts; the legs are greenish yellow.

Immature in foreground with winter adult behind

Calidris alba
SANDERLING
SCOLOPACIDAE 20 cm.

The habitual tide-dodging tactics of the Sanderling relate it much more to Canute than the Knot, with which it shares a 'comfortable' shape and grey appearance in winter, though it is even paler, most of the head and all the under parts being white, while the upper parts are light grey with faint darker markings. The black 'wrist' on the forewing often shows up when the bird is on the ground and is a good distinguishing mark. On the wing the blackish primary coverts contrast with a prominent white wing-bar and the dark centre of the rump and tail show up against their white sides. Juveniles often have a buffish tinge to the breast and back, which is patterned black and pale grey; the crown is also streaked with black. In summer there is a general russet suffusion of the upper parts, head and breast, which is spotted black and usually cleanly defined from the white belly. Some adults, however, show white on the breast and others keep much of the summer plumage into the autumn.

The Sanderling's breeding status in Northern Europe rests on small areas of Svalbard and possibly Franz Josef Land: the whole distribution is high arctic and discontinuous, recalling that

main throughout the northern summer. Passage of adults followed by juveniles reaches its 'autumn' peak in July on British estuaries (23,272 in 1972) and the return peak is in May (26,215 in 1973). Ringing has traced a bird from Iceland (presumably having bred in Greenland) to Norfolk in the following July, while another ringed in April in Britain was recovered in June of the same year at Murmansk in north-western Russia, indicating 2 widely separated sources of the passage flocks. Even more recently, birds dyed on their Greenland breeding grounds have been seen in several British localities the following autumn.

Small parties of Sanderlings skirting the sea's edge are relatively confiding; large flocks, as with other waders, are much less approachable. Often the plump little birds will run ahead of the intruder rather than take wing and fly back past him. Their feeding action has been felicitously described by B. W. Tucker, 'darting over the sand at astonishing speed, like a clockwork toy, and even when picking up food only slowing down enough to allow quick dabs to this side and that'. Much is gleaned from the backwash of the surge: sandhoppers (Gammarids), other small crustaceans, small molluscs, parts of dead fish and medusae, edible plant fragments. The feeding forays by a tight little bunch of birds may be accompanied by a continual twittering, which

OPPOSITE *Winter group*
BELOW *Adult in summer*

of the Knot: parts of the coasts and islands of Siberia, Greenland, arctic Canada and, very locally, Alaska. This makes the appearance of birds in breeding plumage on Scottish hills in recent summers the more surprising. Leaving the tundra areas after about 2 months occupation, Sanderlings almost span the globe to winter from Northern Europe (about 4000 on British estuaries in 1972–3) to South America, including the Falkland Islands, southern Africa, Australia and New Zealand, and intermediately, with sandy rather than muddy beaches their preferred habitat, on which many non-breeders remain

turns into the typical *wit wit* call when they eventually take wing. In summer a good deal of vegetable food is eaten, including plant buds and moss 'fruits', as well as insects when they briefly proliferate.

The Sanderling's song is a loud churring which, to 2 British ornithologists, recalled the reel of the Grasshopper Warbler, *Locustella naevia*. They (C. D. Dalgety and J. H. McNeile) described how the male rose with rapidly vibrating wings to some 5 m. above the ground, then sang as he dived earthwards, though sometimes the flight was prolonged and took the form

of small circles. Males chase females or rival males and display on the ground with wings drooped and feathers puffed out. The chosen breeding area is usually within 3 km. of the coast, on stony but quite well vegetated tundra with dwarf willows and flowering plants, and the nest itself is a small scrape, often partly sheltered, and lined with willow leaves. The clutch of 4 eggs is probably laid daily, from midsummer in Greenland, even later in Siberia. The eggs usually have a dull greenish-olive ground colour; the rather sparse brown markings are concentrated at the broad end. Both parents incubate,

the female probably taking the major share; injury-feigning and rodent-run distraction displays have been recorded from brooding birds. The chicks hatch in about $3\frac{1}{2}$ weeks; they are black and light buff, spotted with white above, whitish below and fledge in about $3\frac{1}{2}$ weeks, attended mainly by one parent. They soon flock, to follow the adults on their long autumn journeys. Studies by D. F. Parmelee and R. B. Payne on Bathurst Island in the Canadian arctic suggest that, as with Temminck's Stint, a proportion of female Sanderlings lay 2 clutches, of which the male incubates one.

Recurvirostra avosetta
AVOCET

RECURVIROSTRIDAE 43 cm. (bill: 8·25 cm.)
The emblem of the Royal Society for the Protection of Birds represents the conspicuous type of wader, like the Oystercatcher and the Vanellid plovers (lapwings), with little seasonal difference in appearance and the sexes looking alike. The black and white plumage of the adult is shown on the plate: on the juvenile the black areas are very dark brown and the white has a brownish tinge. On the ground or in flight, when the black primaries and white tail, with the blue-grey legs projecting well beyond, show up, the Avocet is unmistakable.

Confined to the Old World but highly fragmented, the breeding distribution of the Avocet is relatively southerly. The largest continuous area is from the Balkans across central Asia to about 120°E, similar to that occupied by the Shelduck and Oystercatcher. There are smaller enclaves in Europe, from the North Sea and western Baltic coasts to the Mediterranean and thence, very widely separated, in North, East and South Africa, believed by K. H. Voous to be fairly recent colonizations. The breeding groups in Denmark, the Netherlands and East Anglia have increased in recent years, England (after 2 pairs bred in Ireland in 1938) being recolonized in the 1940s. The North European breeding population was estimated in 1969 at over 10,000 pairs, of which over 4000 pairs and 770 non-breeders were in the Netherlands (S. T. Tjallingii). The preferred habitat, whether inland or coastal, is a shallow saline lagoon with low hummocks for nesting. The northerly breeding areas are deserted in autumn, but about 100 Avocets winter in south-west England, not far from others along the west French coast. The main winter quarters are the salt and alkaline lakes of East Africa where concentrations of 30,000 birds have been reported. Young Avocets ringed in England have been recovered in Spain and Portugal and some probably winter there.

Three other species of avocet are recognized at present, in North and South America and in Australia. Some authorities regard them all as conspecific; they certainly are as distinctive in their habits as their appearance is similar. Their most notable feature is the fine, uptilted bill which they sweep from side to side, as they wade through shallow water, creaming small organisms off the surface and swallowing them with a quick jerk of the head. The head is also dipped in deeper water and Avocets will swim and up-end like ducks. A variety of insects and their larvae, small molluscs and crustaceans, annelid worms, fish fry and spawn are caught by these specialized techniques. After feeding, Avocets often rest on one leg, sit down, or sit up on their tarsi, heads tucked in the scapular feathers. If alarmed, heads are raised and bobbed before taking off into regular beating flight, with the *kluut* call

which is the onomatopoeic Dutch name.

Avocets are gregarious at all times and make social flight movements as well as engaging in displays and fights between groups of pairs, first described by G. F. Makkink. As in the piping choruses of the Oystercatcher, the birds point their bills towards the ground and bow, accompanied by a special, rather metallic *tuc* note. Each pair keeps close together, then moves forward, the birds presenting their flanks to their opponents and trying to buffet them with a wing, often springing up to get in their blow. The combats are interrupted by various distraction displays; their function is to aid both the formation and reinforcement of the pair bond. Avocets are monogamous (though there are cases of more than one female laying in the same nest) and mate after elaborate preparations, during which the female crouches with neck stretched along the surface of the water and the male makes 'preening' movements as he approaches, finally jumping on to her back. After mating, he leaves a wing over her back and the birds run forward with bills crossed before separating.

On the colonial breeding grounds the Avocet develops a repertoire of hostile cries, one apparently specially against gulls, and attacks all intruders, which is probably why Kentish Plovers often nest in proximity. The Avocets' nests may be only a few metres apart on low mounds and consist of a bare scrape or of a substantial structure of dead vegetation, mostly accumulated by the birds' 'straw-tossing' displays, though it may be built up if the water level rises on the lagoon after heavy rain. The 3 to 5 eggs are like poorly marked Lapwings' eggs and are laid from mid-April onwards. Both sexes incubate them and their graceful changeover has been captured by many bird-photographers. The downy young hatch in 22 to 24 days and are very vulnerable at first, in spite of both parents vociferously attending them. Fledging takes about 6 weeks and then parties form near the breeding ground before moving away.

The recolonization of East Anglia by the Avocet has given the RSPB a remarkable opportunity for environmental management to the bird's advantage. The output of young fluctuates violently from year to year; at the largest colony, on Havergate Island, 86 pairs reared only 6 young in 1974, but 107 pairs raised 80 young in 1975, a year when the total English population, at 157 pairs, was the highest on record. The chief threats to the young are predators, inclement weather and lack of suitable food, the last 2 being often related. Large gulls are the worst avian predators, killing 40 chicks in 1975. The salinity of water in the Havergate lagoons can be regulated to encourage the ragworm *Nereis* and crustaceans *Corophium* and *Palaemonetes*. Insects are also very important, and abundance of chironomid midge larvae was probably the main factor in the good 'production' of young Avocets in 1975.

Adults

Phalaropus fulicarius
GREY PHALAROPE
PHALAROPODIDAE 20 cm.

Among waders equal sharing of parental duties is characteristic; but there is a minority tendency, mainly among species with rather bright breeding plumages, for the sex role to be reversed and for the males to sit on the eggs and rear the young unaided. The phalaropes, a family of only 3 species, show this behaviour; they are also untypical in swimming rather than wading, using their partially webbed feet and coot-like (hence *fulicarius*) lobed toes, in their complete seasonal change of plumage, and in wintering at sea. Two of the 3 species breed in Northern Europe; the third and largest, Wilson's Phalarope, *Phalaropus tricolor*, which breeds inland in North America, is now known to be a fairly regular vagrant.

The Grey Phalarope in summer plumage is one of the most striking of all waders and the female, who lacks brood patches, is both larger and considerably brighter than the male. Breeding birds begin to moult early in July and, by the time they take to the sea again at the end of the month, the males are half-way to winter plumage. This is predominantly grey and white; the sexes are alike and can be told from the Sanderling, the only other small European wader that looks white in winter, by the rather irregular dark grey patch round the eye. Phalaropes also appear much slimmer, almost attenuated, and their habits are quite distinctive; differences between the 2 species are given under the Red-necked Phalarope.

The breeding distribution of the Grey Phalarope is far northern: the tundra and river valleys of coastal Siberia, Alaska, arctic Canada and parts of west and east Greenland. The European stations are Novaya Zemlya, Svalbard, Bear Island and Iceland, where the birds are most accessible but very local. They arrive in spring in large flocks, braving the still icy conditions, and these flocks reform after breeding. On autumn passage Grey Phalaropes appear regularly, sometimes in large numbers, in the Western Approaches and off the Bay of Biscay, while small numbers occur on both sides of the North Sea; but they are rare in spring. The winter quarters were for a long time a mystery. Birds turn up as far south as New Zealand, South Africa and the Falkland Islands off South America, but the main areas are concentrated offshore, one off the coast of northern Chile and the other in the Atlantic between 10° and 25°N, about 160 km. from the Cape Verde Islands and Cape Blanco.

Another peculiarity of the phalaropes, what B. W. Tucker called their 'well-known trick of spinning round and round on the surface', has been variously diagnosed as a form of display or, which now seems established, a method of stirring up surface plankton at sea and 'quiescent mosquito larvae' in shallow pools, so that the bird can pick them up with its fine bill. It also dips its head and up-ends like a duck, snaps flying insects in the air and feeds on land like a more normal wader. The diet in summer and on passage is mainly small crustaceans and molluscs, some insect larvae and adults, and a little vegetable matter.

Conspicuous indifference to man is another phalarope trait. When induced to fly a short way, the Grey Phalarope moves erratically, but on longer flights beats fast and regularly like other waders. It swims buoyantly, bobs its head like a Moorhen (Tucker) and stretches its neck with bill held horizontally when alert (A. A. Kistchinski). The usual call is a low-pitched *whit* or *cruit*, disyllabic on the breeding ground, where Kistchinski also noted a quick *tchirr-lyk* of excitement. The aggressive posture is much the same on land or water: feathers ruffled, head sunk between shoulders and bill pointed forward at the opponent, who is usually of the same sex. Females are expectedly the more aggressive, and the incubating male has a special 'driving flight' to get rid of females near the nest. He 'shivers' in the air with legs and tail hanging, then attacks the intruder, beating her with his wings until she leaves.

OPPOSITE *Summer adults, female in foreground, male behind*
BELOW *Adult in winter*

In courtship the female makes a circling display flight, showing off her white underwings and calling *cruit*. Sometimes several hens pursue one cock. Before mating, the pair may swim in close contact, touching each other with their bills; they also do this on land. Either sex, but more often the female, may rise in the air alone and rattle its wings. Kistchinski found that the pair bond at most persisted only to the egg-laying stage. Sometimes mating seems to be promiscuous.

Grey Phalaropes, whether nesting in small groups or individually, show no territorial sense.

Several scrapes may be formed in the tundra vegetation, usually close to a small pool, sometimes on the shore of a lake or the sea. One is lined with local vegetation and receives, from early June to July according to latitude, 4 buff to umber, pear-shaped eggs, boldly marked with darker browns. The male begins to sit on the second or third egg. Incubation lasts at least $2\frac{1}{2}$ weeks and the young fledge in between 2 and 3 weeks. According to Kistchinski they are then abandoned by the males and stay by small pools for several weeks before going down to the shore.

Phalaropus lobatus
RED-NECKED PHALAROPE
PHALAROPODIDAE 16·5 cm.

Although scarcer as a visitor on passage, this species has a far wider European breeding range than the Grey Phalarope. The summer plumages of the 2 are absolutely distinct and, as with its relative, the female Red-necked is more brightly coloured than the male, who tends to have more buff streaks on the back and less 'red' – really orange – on his neck. In winter the 2 species are very much alike. Both have blackish legs and bills, but the partial webbing on the Grey Phalarope's feet retains its yellow tint and so may the base of the female's bill. Much more distinctive is the broad, rather flattened shape of the Grey's bill as opposed to the 'needle-fine' organ of the Red-necked Phalarope. Generally, the Red-necked's plumage is darker, with more streaking on the upper parts and a more showy whitish wing-bar; it is also considerably smaller than the Grey, though this does not help identification unless there is some standard of comparison. The juvenile has buff streaks on its blackish back and is whiter on the head than the Grey Phalarope, with 'breast more or less tinged vinous' (B. W. Tucker).

The holarctic breeding range is similar to but more southerly than that of the Grey Phalarope. In Europe the Red-necked is rare in Svalbard and absent from Bear Island, but nests commonly in Iceland, over much of Norway, in the north of Sweden, Finland and Russia and in some of the Baltic states. It holds on precariously in Shetland and the Scottish Hebrides and in one west Irish locality, probably its most southerly breeding station in the world. The almost continuous decline of the Red-necked Phalarope in these outposts of its range is in contrast to the southward spread of several northern species, including waders such as the Wood Sandpiper and Temminck's Stint, which has been a feature of British bird distribution in recent years. There seem to be no obvious local factors to account for it, although disturbance by man and grazing animals may have had some effect. The habitat ranges from tundra to the eutrophic lochs of the Hebridean machair, northern birchwoods and subalpine moorland. Birds on passage occur all over northern Europe on the way to the winter concentrations at sea. One of these is in the Gulf of Oman and the northern part of the Arabian Sea; others are believed to be in the Pacific north of New Guinea, off the coast of Peru not far from one of the Grey Phalarope wintering areas, and off the West African coast.

In general habits the Red-necked resembles the Grey Phalarope: short, erratic flights, swimming and 'spinning' on the water, and remarkable tameness: a male has been photographed brooding the young in a human hand. The food in summer seems to consist mainly of insects and their larvae taken from the water or from riparian vegetation; also small molluscs and worms. At sea no doubt this species is sustained

like its relative by the teeming surface zooplankton. The usual call is *whit*, similar to but lower pitched than that of the Grey Phalarope. Its vocabulary appears to be larger, probably because of more observation on the breeding ground; and the breeding season displays were the subject of one of N. Tinbergen's first detailed field studies, in Greenland in 1934. There is a variously rendered disyllabic alarm call. The hen rises into 'ceremonial flight' crying *wit wit wit wit*, then calls *wedu wedu wedu* when she settles; a rapid repeated note is used by both sexes in the 'scrape ceremony' and by the female after laying.

The aggressive posture is closely similar to that of the Grey Phalarope, which may attack this species, as it may itself attack Sanderlings

OPPOSITE *Summer adults, female in foreground, male behind*
BELOW *Adult in winter*

and Turnstones. The male's driving flight when 'defending' the nest against females also occurs but apparently more rarely. A. A. Kistchinski considers that the 'ceremonial flight' described by Tinbergen corresponds to the 'circling flight' of the female Grey Phalarope; and both species rattle their wings in display. The female also rattles or whirrs her wings briefly after rising almost erect on the water with neck bent forward; this may be followed by chasing the male. The ceremonial flight stops when the pair has formed; the female invites the male to mate by wing-rattling and then lying on the water, tail

towards the male, who may rattle in response, take wing and copulate, nearly submerging the female. Coition may also take place at the nest (B. Hantzsch). 'Scraping' by both sexes follows pairing, with breast on the ground and tail in the air and various ritual actions, including pecking in the scrape and the male tossing grass stems over his shoulder.

According to Tinbergen both sexes line the chosen scrape, which is often near water and may be quite well hidden in a tussock, under dwarf willows or even taller vegetation. Several pairs usually nest near together and sometimes

large colonies form. Eggs are laid from late May in Britain to the third week of June in the extreme north of the range. The usual clutch is 4, rather glossier than eggs of the Grey Phalarope but with the same range of ground colour and heavy dark brown markings, though minutely and lightly spotted types occur. The female lays at intervals of up to 36 hours and the male then takes over incubation. The eggs hatch after about 20 days and the young fly in $2\frac{1}{2}$ to 3 weeks. Several observers have recorded males feigning injury when disturbed from the nest or the brood.

113

Stercorarius skua
GREAT SKUA
STERCORARIIDAE 58 cm.

This, in human terms, ugly and rapacious creature has, until taxonomists decide otherwise, the unique distinction of being the only bird species to nest both within the arctic (Bear Island in 1970) and antarctic circles, where it is also the only vertebrate animal, apart from man and his sleigh dogs, to have reached the South Pole, though the race *maccormicki* that achieves this is often given separate specific status from the 3 other races inhabiting the southern hemisphere.

The Great Skua or Bonxie is between a Great Black-backed and a Herring Gull in size, dark brown with tawny streaks above, lighter below and with a whitish patch at the base of the primaries which shows on both sides of the wing. Its body is stocky and powerful, its bill, wings and tail relatively shorter than a large gull's. The juvenile plumage is a more uniform brown, with less white on the wing. Great Skuas mature when 3 years old.

Apart from the Bear Island record, the northern and nominate race *skua* breeds only in Iceland, the Faeroe Islands and the extreme north of Scotland, including Shetland, Orkney and the Outer Hebrides. After breeding, the birds disperse gradually southwards; the wintering area seems to be mainly in the north Atlantic, percolating into the western Mediterranean, though Shetland-ringed birds have reached Guyana and Brazil, south of the equator. They have also been recovered inland in Europe as far as 34°E, while in summer a 2-year-old British-ringed bird turned up in west Greenland. On the other hand, birds of the southern races have crossed the equator, reaching the West Indies and even Japan.

When not aroused, Great Skuas look clumsy, suitable only for the scavenging, which probably provides most of their living, whether it is refuse from ships or carrion on the shore; like all skuas, they can fish for themselves when necessary. The dramatic moments come when one or a pair of Bonxies pursues another sea bird to deprive it either of its catch or of its life. A Gannet may be seized by its wing-tip until it disgorges, and many species down to a tern may be attacked. In a chase to the death the skua follows every move of its victim with remarkable agility, then closes in to strike it several times, finally bringing it to the sea where it is dispatched and eaten. The southern races are the scourge of the penguin colonies.

Great Skuas often settle on the sea, and visit fresh water to bathe and preen; 'clubs' form near pools and become so well established that they can be located by the green of the enriched vegetation. The commonest display may be seen at a 'club': the bird raises its wings with the tips slanting backwards, stretches its neck with bill held downwards and utters a loud *hah hah hah*. This can also be the prelude to courtship, when the male parades before the female with fluffed neck, and mating may follow. There is also a bowing ceremony and a display flight with a special call.

The Bonxie breeds in scattered pairs over bare heather or grass moorland; the territories are fiercely defended, the birds sweeping in to attack at low level, but usually sheering away from a human intruder at the last moment. The nest is a large grass-lined cup in which 2 stone to reddish-brown eggs, usually marked with darker spots and blotches, are laid from mid-May onwards. Both sexes share the incubation for 28 to 30 days. The chicks hatch in light brown down and fledge in 6 to 7 weeks, closely attended by the parents.

Operation Seafarer recorded about 3170 pairs in Scotland in 1969–70, of which more than half were on Foula, a Shetland outlier. In Iceland F. Guðmundsson estimated 7200 pairs in 1954 but there has been a considerable decrease since; the Faeroe population was about 500 pairs in 1970.

Stercorarius pomarinus
POMARINE SKUA
STERCORARIIDAE 43 cm. (central tail feathers project 5 to 7·5 cm.)

Largest of the 3 small skuas, the Pomarine occurs in a scarcer nearly uniform dark brown phase and a commoner light phase in which yellowish cheeks and collar separate the blackish crown from the dark grey-brown upper parts, underwing and under tail coverts; throat, breast and belly are white and a pale area shows on the wing in flight. The adults' unique feature is the elongation of the central tail feathers which are blunt-ended and twisted. Juveniles, with short tails, are dark brown with light barring, especially on the under parts, and cannot be told from juvenile Arctic Skuas except on size.

The Pomarine Skua breeds on Svalbard (rare) and from the Kanin Peninsula in north-west Russia round the Arctic at about 70°N to Canada, where its range becomes fragmented, and west Greenland; its habitat is the bare tundra. The main wintering areas are oceanic, off the west coast of Africa and off New South Wales in Australia; a small spring migration in the British area has recently been detected (D. L. Davenport). In summer the main food is the lemming, hunted from the air or on foot and, to the exclusion of the Long-tailed Skua (W. J. Maher), supplemented by small waders and their eggs, and carrion. Later the Pomarine becomes piratical; it can kill birds as big as Black-headed Gulls.

The display reveals the function of the twisted rectrices: when the tail is fanned they are arched upwards to form an apex, while the head is thrown back and the breast fluffed out (F. A. Pitelka, F. Salomonsen). The usual call is a sharp *which-yew*. Pairs nest scattered widely over the tundra, laying 2 olive to brown eggs, with dark markings, in a bare scrape from mid-June. Both sexes incubate; the pale brown chicks hatch in about 4 weeks and can fly in 5 to 6 weeks, while still in parental care.

Great Skua adult (right); Pomarine Skuas, immature bird (above centre), light phase adult (below centre) and dark phase adult (left)

Stercorarius parasiticus
ARCTIC SKUA
STERCORARIIDAE 38 cm. (central tail feathers project a further 6·5 to 7·5 cm.)

The best known and most widely distributed of the skuas or, in America, jaegers, has 2 plumage phases which are still in contention over much of its range and produce many intermediate forms. Typical birds of each phase are shown on the plate. In flight a pale patch shows on the wings of both phases. The dark phase predominates in the Baltic area (95 per cent of the small Finnish population) and varies from 80 to 50 per cent in Scotland and the Faeroe Islands. The proportion of light birds increases to 40 per cent in north Iceland, 90 per cent in north Norway and nearly 100 per cent in Svalbard and Greenland. Working with the Fair Isle (Shetland) colony, P. O'Donald and J. W. F. Davis suggest that the pale phase is genetically at an advantage and will eventually replace the perhaps more primitive dark phase. Juveniles, which lack the long pointed central feathers of the wedge-shaped tail, are variably mottled and barred with dark and light brown. They do not breed until they are about 4 years old.

The breeding range of the Arctic Skua is practically continuous round the northern hemisphere, mainly between 60° and 70°N, with a southward extension in the Pacific, and north to Franz Josef Land, so that it overlaps the Pomarine Skua: their coastal tundra habitat is much the same and there may be interspecific competition. In winter this species is oceanic, following the Arctic Tern on its southward migration down to about 30° to 50°S but not into antarctic waters. Birds are therefore seen offshore in many parts of Northern Europe where they do not breed; in 1972-3 there was an August peak of 65 in the Wash in eastern England.

Rakish but elegant are anthropomorphic terms suggested by Arctic Skuas as they chase a variety of seabirds, from Gannets to, especially, Kittiwakes and terns. Frequently 2 cooperate, seeming to take it in turns to harry the victim and catch the prize as it is dropped or disgorged, to be swallowed on the wing or on the water. The attackers are usually silent, the attacked vociferous. Skuas can fish for themselves; they also kill small birds, with repeated strikes like a Great Skua, and mammals, and eat eggs, carrion, insects, spiders and berries.

On the breeding ground, where they nest in loose colonies, often among their favourite victims, Arctic Terns, and gulls, Arctic Skuas display in flight, diving down, sweeping upward, tumbling and turning. On the ground the male dances round the female, who hisses at him with open bill (B. Hantzch). The usual cry is remarkably like the Kittiwake's onomatopoeic call on the ledges, and accompanies the intense distraction display, as the birds fling themselves about,

usually on an eminence in sight of the intruder. But they also attack with determination and a menacing ticking call, sometimes actually striking home. The nest site may be 'traditional', with a look-out post close by, a bare scrape in the moor or tundra; 2 eggs, greenish to brown in colour, spotted and blotched with umber, are laid 48 hours apart from late May onwards. Both sexes, which frequently remate and may be of either phase, incubate the eggs for 3½ to 4 weeks. The dark brown downy chicks hatch and are tended separately, the parents feeding them for some weeks. They can fly at about 4 weeks but may not be fully independent for another month.

Skuas when breeding can be fairly accurately counted and Operation Seafarer gave the British total, all in Scotland, as 1090 pairs in 1969-70, making it the 'least numerous sea-bird breeding regularly in Britain and Ireland'; there may be competition from the increasing Great Skua.

Stercorarius longicaudus
LONG-TAILED SKUA
STERCORARIIDAE 46 cm. (central tail feathers may project a further 12 to 20 cm.)

The smallest and most graceful of the skuas is described by its prominent feature, the remarkably elongated and whippy central rectrices. But there is some overlap with long-feathered Arctic Skuas and other characters have to be considered, as summarized by B. W. Tucker: 'no pectoral band . . . little or no whitish on underside of wing, back somewhat paler and greyer . . . forming sharper contrast with nearly black crown . . . legs grey or blue grey', instead of the Arctic Skua's black. There is an exceptionally rare dark plumaged form. Juveniles are generally greyer than Arctics, but are hard to distinguish in the field; both show white on the wing.

The Long-tailed Skua's breeding range is similar to the Arctic Skua's but less extensive, with a gap from Iceland to the Baltic area. In some recent summers odd birds have stayed among Arctic Skuas on Fair Isle. The breeding areas are often on tundra some way inland and birds turn up far from the sea on passage, which is, however, mainly offshore, making this the scarcest skua in North European coastal waters. The most important wintering area is in South American waters; 1500 birds have been reported off Argentina in November.

Long-tailed Skuas swim buoyantly with tails raised and have a rather tern-like flight, often hovering to pick food off the surface. They are less piratical than other skuas, and are dependent on the lemming for a successful breeding season; they also take rats, mice, small birds like the Snow Bunting, *Plectrophenax nivalis*, and many insects (W. J. Maher), fish offal and berries. The usual call is rendered *kree kree*, but there are apparently special notes when attacking bird or mammal intruders and a long call

proclaiming territorial rights. Another call is used in the 3 distinct ritual display-flights. The tail feathers are raised in ground display.

Breeding habits resemble those of other small skuas, but the clutch may vary from 1 to 3 eggs according to the food supply. These are laid at 1½- to 2-day intervals and hatch after 23 days incubation by both sexes. The grey-brown downy chicks hatch at intervals and separate, though tended by both parents. They can fly when about 3 weeks old.

Adult Arctic Skuas, light phase (below), dark phase (centre). Adult Long-tailed Skua (above)

Larus marinus
GREAT BLACK-BACKED GULL
LARIDAE 63 to 69 cm. (wing-span about 1·5 m.)

The 'G. B-B.' as it is called by bird-watchers, is the largest and most powerful gull breeding in Northern Europe, though the Glaucous Gull runs it close and there is probably competition where their ranges overlap. In spite of its size, this species can be difficult to tell from the dark-mantled race of the Lesser Black-backed Gull, but the pallid, usually flesh-coloured legs are distinctive. In flight the wing-beat is measurably slower than that of Herring Gull or Lesser Black-back. The brown-plumaged juvenile already shows a darker back and wings with a paler head and under parts than the Herring Gull and this difference increases in the immature plumages, third-year birds being nearly as adults but with dark barring on the tail. They are mature when 4 years old. Adults in winter show some brown streaks on the head in contrast to the 'intolerably white' breast of Alasdair Maclean's poem.

The breeding distribution of the Great Black-back is essentially North Atlantic, down to 40°N on the east coast of North America (a comparatively recent extension) and to Brittany in Europe; the northern limits are in west Greenland, Bear Island and Svalbard (rare); and eastward along the Scandinavian coast to the Kolguev Peninsula in Russia. The breeding habitat is high or low rocky coast with offshore stacks and islands, with some colonies on inland lakes, as in Sweden, Iceland and Ireland, or on moorland in Britain; the low-lying North Sea shores are therefore only favoured in autumn and winter, 10 estuaries on the British east coast holding some 20,000 birds in 1972-3. There is a southward dispersal after breeding, largely of juvenile and immature birds, as far as the sub-tropics; British-ringed birds have been recovered in Iberia, while birds from both Russia and Iceland have been recorded in Britain and Ireland.

Outside the breeding season large gulls apparently divide their time between bouts of rapacious feeding and long periods of inactivity, when parties of mixed species stand or sit on rocks, shores, buildings or the water. This may be partly due to the easy living of those who follow fishing boats or frequent harbours and refuse dumps and are therefore most readily observed. Away from man's direct influence living is likely to be sterner and more time spent in search of food. The G. B-B. will take anything from a sickly lamb (alive or dead) to a flying ant, and is noted for its attacks in the breeding season on the colonial Manx Shearwater, Puffin and Little Auk, pouncing on birds as they enter or quit their breeding holes and often leaving the skin of the victim inside-out; it will kill many other birds, and a range of small mammals and fish, and take starfish, molluscs, crustaceans, worms and insects; some vegetable matter, especially grain, is also eaten. It will usually see off other gulls and sometimes rob them like a skua.

The deep *agh agh agh* call and repeated expletive *owk* of the Great Black-back stand out from the cacophony of a mixed gull assembly. There is also a 'long call' used to 'advertise' presence and territory. The displays have a general similarity to those of the much more studied Herring and Lesser Black-backed Gulls.

The typical Great Black-back nest is on a prominent stack or eminence in a mixed gull colony, a literal demonstration of its dominant position, and many pairs breed away from their fellows. But colonies of a thousand and more pairs do form, for example on the islands at the mouth of the Norwegian Varanger Fjord, in Orkney, and on North Rona, the Hebridean outlier where later in the year the G. B-B.s scavenge the Grey Seal breeding colony. The nest, built by both sexes, may be a large pile of grass, other local plants, twigs, seaweed and litter, though sometimes only a sparsely-lined scrape in peat or among rocks is made. The 2 or 3 large pale buff or olive-brown eggs, spotted and blotched with dark brown and underlying ashy marks, are laid from mid-April in the south. Incubation starts before completion of the clutch and is shared by the parents. The chicks, in grey-brown down with blackish spots, hatch in up to 4 weeks and leave the nest to hide in surrounding vegetation after a few days. They fledge in 7 or 8 weeks but may pester adults for food for much longer.

Operation Seafarer estimated the British and Irish coastal breeding population at some 22,000 pairs in 1969-70, of which 16,000 were in Scotland. This makes it probably the least numerous of the 6 gulls breeding regularly in the area, where it has, however been steadily increasing during the twentieth century, probably due to food indirectly supplied by man; because of its predation on other seabirds control methods have been applied, for example in Dyfed (South Wales) but the increase goes on. A characteristic of the Great Black-back is the occupation by pairs of possible nesting sites without breeding, sometimes in seabird colonies outside its present range, an indication of impending spread.

Adult in foreground, immature behind

Larus fuscus
LESSER BLACK-BACKED GULL
LARIDAE 53 cm.

This and the next species form part of a species chain whose unravelling provides endless occupation for systematic ornithologists. In Northern Europe there are 2 races which have relatively 'black' backs, the nominate *fuscus* or Scandinavian Lesser Black-backed Gull, whose mantle is almost as dark as that of the Great Black-back, and the 'British' *graellsii*, in which the area is slate-grey, lightest on the mantle, darkest towards the white-edged wing-tips, a division which shows up clearly in flight. In other respects both resemble rather refined Herring Gulls (see plates) but have yellow legs. In winter their heads are streaked with brown. The juvenile plumage is brown, with dark primaries and dark-centred feathers, especially on the upper parts; the legs are pale pinkish and the bill blackish with a light base. There is a gradual differentiation with age between the dark mantle and the rest of the plumage, which is practically white by the second summer, though maturity is not reached until the fourth summer.

K. H. Voous, whose views have generally been followed in this book, combines with these 2 races all the yellow-legged races of light-backed 'Herring Gulls' (and the pink-legged form from north-east Siberia). The breeding range of the 2 dark-backed races runs from south-east Iceland (colonized about 50 years ago), the Faeroe Islands, Britain, Ireland, and the coast of western Europe intermittently from Brittany to northern Scandinavia and the Baltic. If the yellow-legged Herring Gulls are included, the distribution is extended right across Eurasia roughly between 65° and 75°N, with a southern branch to that central Asian region where several other usually coastal birds (Shelduck, Oystercatcher, Avocet) also nest, and this is connected with local groups in the Mediterranean region and the Atlantic islands.

The breeding habitat of the Lesser Black-back *sensu stricto* may be coastal on cliffs and islands, or inland on moors, tundra, river and lakesides; exceptionally the British race nests on buildings. There is a little interbreeding between Lesser Black-backs and pink-legged Herring Gulls both in Britain and the Netherlands and their hybrids are fertile; but generally the 2 species keep to themselves in separate colonies. Lesser Black-backs are primarily summer visitors to their breeding grounds and dark-mantled birds are seen in the British area on passage. But since about 1945 British, with a few Scandinavian, Lesser Black-backs have wintered increasingly in Britain. Numbers rose from hundreds to 7000 in about 1965 and must now be very much higher. The attraction is the amount of edible refuse available round large towns. The majority that still migrate go to the Atlantic coasts of Iberia and North Africa but a few penetrate much further south.

Especially in the breeding season, Lesser Black-backs are relatively 'natural' feeders, preying upon other birds and their eggs, taking fish, many crustaceans and marine worms, some molluscs, earthworms and carrion, also grain in summer. But they frequently follow ships away from the shore and attend fishing boats. In winter, as described, a proportion of British Lesser Black-backs have become full-time scavengers, associating with other species which, on the whole, they do not in summer.

The usual calls of the Lesser Black-back and Herring Gull, corresponding to the *owk* and *agh agh agh* of the Great Black-back, are rendered *keew* and *hahaha* by N. Tinbergen. Both are hoarser when uttered by the Lesser Black-back, which makes much use of the *keew* and little of the *hahaha*. The position is reversed with the Herring Gull and Tinbergen points out the importance of this in the evolution of 2 distinct species. Some forms of display are also still common, notably the 'upright threat position' with neck tensely stretched and bill pointing downward, a prelude to actual buffeting with the wing or pecking at the opponent. There are also displacement activities: the violent pulling up of material in simulation of nest-building and the scraping at the ground accompanying 'choking' (see Herring Gull). These actions can be shared by closely related species because they do not compromise their identity; it is biologically preferable, however, that call notes and other means of identification should be distinct.

Breeding colonies of the Lesser Black-back, picked out by green perching mounds, may spread over large areas of moorland or be concentrated in the vegetation cap of an island shared with Herring Gulls. The Black-backs tend to nest in thick cover, leaving the splash zones and rocky outcrops to their relatives. The nest itself, built by both sexes, varies from a pile of grass and debris, heather and moss, to a nearly bare scrape. The 2 or 3 greenish-blue to dark brown eggs, usually spotted and streaked with blackish brown and ashy markings, cannot be told from Herring Gull's eggs and are laid from late April in the south. Incubation by both parents starts before the clutch is complete and the young, again indistinguishable from Herring Gulls in their grey-brown, black streaked down, hatch in up to 4 weeks and fledge, with both parents attending them, in 4 or 5 weeks.

Operation Seafarer's estimate of the coastal breeding population of Britain and Ireland in 1969-70 was 47,000 pairs, with an enormous colony of 17,500 pairs on dunes at Walney, Cumbria. In general there is a history of increase in recent years except where Lesser Black-backs have come into competition with Great Black-backs or, as in Orkney and Shetland, with Great Skuas.

Adult (left) and immature (right)

Larus argentatus
HERRING GULL
LARIDAE 56 cm.

Two races of large light-mantled gulls breed in Northern Europe, the nominate *argentatus* with flesh-pink legs, and the yellow-legged *omissus* which, as discussed under the Lesser Black-backed Gull, is lumped by K. H. Voous with that species. However, it is perhaps better considered here since, apart from their different leg colour, both forms are more or less identical in habits and plumage, though *omissus* has a slightly darker mantle. Their larger size, powerful yellow bill with a red spot on the gonys or angle of the lower mandible, and pale eyes distinguish them from the smaller, brown-eyed Common Gull, which has greenish legs. But the Common Gull's wing-tips are also black with white terminal mirrors and in flight, with no size comparison, confusion is certainly possible. Juvenile Herring Gulls of any race are almost indistinguishable from Lesser Black-backs but can be told from juvenile Common Gulls not only on size but by their all-brown barred tails, the smaller species having a well defined dark terminal band. Full Herring Gull plumage is attained in 3 years with gradual reduction of the brown; adults in winter have brown streaks on head and neck.

Herring Gulls of the race *argentatus* breed from Iceland (colonized 1927), Bear Island (1932 but since vacated) and Svalbard (1950), the Faeroe Islands, Britain and Ireland, and north-western Europe to Scandinavia and the Baltic area, where they are also recent arrivals in strength. Voous believes *argentatus* to be an off-shoot of the pink-legged North American *smithsonianus*, which breeds throughout Canada and into the north-eastern US, and to have been successful in Europe against *L. fuscus* because of its slightly greater size and general adaptability. The race *omissus* breeds in northern Scandinavia and north-western Russia and hybridizes freely with the advancing *argentatus*, which is normally resident, with some dispersal from its most northerly stations. Its breeding habitat is primarily marine, on rocky coasts and cliffs, sand dunes and, increasingly, in British towns and ports on buildings and other artefacts; also by inland lakes, but much less often than the Lesser Black-back on moorland.

To laymen Herring Gulls are probably the typical seagulls, background voices to maritime broadcasts, whatever the ocean. They fly, spells of flapping alternating with long glides and heads turning expectantly to notice possible food sources, over seaside resorts, over wild, surge-battered coastlines, and inland, where in some areas they are assiduous followers of the plough. The food taken is various in kind and varies regionally in popularity. Herring Gulls are scavengers in chief, killers of small birds, including the young of their own species, and of small mammals which they swallow whole; egg-

stealers; pirates on fish-laden Puffins; fishermen in their own right, capable of quite deep diving; scoffers of shore life; gleaners of grain and root crops, and one of the long list of birds that eat earthworms, luring them upwards by pattering with their feet. These tastes are pursued socially and in company with other species of gull, not without fights or chases over prize items of offal or refuse. An unusual feeding habit, shared in Northern Europe with some other gulls and crows, *Corvus* species, is the dropping of shell-fish or crabs from a height to break them. But it does not occur to the gulls initially to drop them on to hard surfaces and success may only be achieved after constant repetition: 39 attempts by one immature bird watched by Niko Tinbergen.

As well as economic enquiries into its food, the Herring Gull has been the subject of a classic behaviour study by Tinbergen, enshrined in his book *A Herring Gull's World* (1953). He analysed the vocabulary of calls, of which the 'general purpose' *keew* and *hahaha* of alarm were mentioned under Lesser Black-backed Gull. 'Loud and staccato', the *keew* is used when attacking a predator; multisyllabic, it becomes the trumpeting or 'long' call, most frequently heard in the breeding season. Then there is the mew used with the young, and the 'choking' *huoh huoh huoh huoh*, uttered with head pointed downward and jerked rhythmically.

On returning to the breeding colony early in spring, individual gulls are able to recognize each other, and old pairs often re-form and may occupy the same territory. New pairs are formed at the 'clubs' of unmated birds, the female usually making the first advance by circling a male, pointing her bill and tossing her head. He may react hostilely or give the 'friendly' mew call; but in any case pair formation is a slow process. The bond is cemented by courtship feeding and, externally, the pair defend their territory against other Herring Gulls and join in chasing predators. The nest is built by both sexes and is similar to that of the other big gulls, though more substantial on a cliff ledge or roof top than when on the ground among sand dunes. The 2 or 3 eggs, indistinguishable from those of the Lesser Black-back, are laid from mid-April in the south and incubated by both parents before the clutch is complete. Tinbergen found that pairs cannot recognize their own eggs, but learn to recognize their downy chicks, which hatch in 28 to 33 days, during the first 5 days out of the egg, when they are being brooded for much of the time. Once this has happened, all strange young are attacked. Adults also prey on other territories, so the safest are those with objects against which the chicks can hide. Those that survive these internecine and other attacks fledge in about 6 weeks but accompany the eventually unwilling parents for much longer. When being fed as chicks, Tinbergen showed that they pecked at the red spot on the parent's gonys, thus inducing it to regurgitate.

Adult (above) and second year immature (below)

Larus canus
COMMON GULL
LARIDAE 41 cm.

British ornithologists agree that the English name of this species is inappropriate but seem unable to accept the American name Mew Gull, perhaps because of its tautonomy, since mew is an old name for gull, surviving in the Dutch *meeuw* and German *Möwe*. Unless a size comparison is possible, distant Common Gulls can be mistaken for Herring Gulls owing to their same general livery, and confused with Black-headed Gulls in winter, especially on the ground where the dissimilar wing patterns are not visible. Close-up, the dark eyes, lack of a bright spot on the more slender greenish-yellow bill, and legs of the same colour are obvious differences from the larger species; the rather darker mantle and the wing-tips, black with white mirrors, are subtler distinctions. The juvenile Common Gull broadly resembles juveniles of the larger species, but the whiter tail-base throws the dark terminal band into greater relief. By the first winter much of the adult plumage has been acquired except on wings and tail; in its first full summer the immature bird has lost more of the brown on its wings; in its second summer, when it may start breeding, the black primary coverts are the chief distinction. There are prominent brown streaks on the head in all winter plumages.

The breeding distribution of the Common Gull extends from Iceland (first record 1955), the Faeroe Islands, Ireland and Scotland (very local in England and Wales) across the continent between 50° and 70°N into Asia and over the Bering Strait to take in a large area of Alaska and north-east Canada, considered by K. H. Voous to be a recent spread; further south and west it is replaced by the Ring-billed Gull, *L. delawarensis*, which has also been sited in Europe. Although nesting on rocky islands, headlands and beaches, the Common Gull breeds extensively inland, not only on lakes and by rivers but on tundra and moorland up to 1500 m. In Europe there are recent records from Poland and Switzerland and in Asia presumed relict areas in the Caucasus and by the Caspian Sea.

After breeding there is a general move south and west, taking European birds into Africa to about 25°N, Asian birds to Indo-China and American birds to California. But ringing returns suggest that almost all British and Irish breeding birds winter within these countries, their numbers swelled by Scandinavian and Baltic visitors; some 200,000 roosted on British and Irish estuaries in 1972-3 (half of them on the Solway Firth) and, in 1963, 125,000 were roosting inland in England alone. Holland's winter population comes also from Scandinavia, and from Germany. The return migration north-east in spring is relatively speedy, but many immature birds remain behind (J. D. R. Vernon).

The general pattern of Common Gull activity in winter is to spread out over arable land and pasture in daytime, retiring to roost in the comparative safety of an estuary or large inland water. The birds hunt worms in the churned-up turf of football and other games pitches as well as following the plough, often mixing with Black-headed Gulls, with whom some have recently been seen flight-feeding over ragwort in the Hebrides (A. W. and L. S. Ewing) evidently after adult insects, an important summer food. The wide range of items taken covers carrion, including traffic victims – a penchant sometimes also fatal to the gull – fish, small birds struck down in flight, eggs and nestlings, defoliating larvae on trees, shellfish, prey taken from other birds, from smaller gulls to Eiders, and a good deal of plant material: berries, roots and seeds. Common Gulls are not, however, great haunters of rubbish dumps or followers of ships and Vernon and T. P. Walsh, who studied them on a playing field, found them comparatively peaceful. They seldom dive, but swim as competently as other gulls, perch frequently on trees as well as posts and buildings, and fly over land and sea with steady beats, in flocks or small parties.

Behaviour in the breeding season has been studied by Uli Weidmann. At first much time is spent feeding, bathing, preening and sleeping, with periodic mass flights ('dreads') away from the colony. The males establish territories and deter rivals by an upright threat posture with wings slightly lifted and ready for action. Females are not repelled and one is eventually accepted and may beg for food, the male sometimes reciprocating. Other displays are related to those observed among Herring and Black-headed Gulls, such as the 'long call', 'choking', and 'head flagging'. The *kyow* call can be recognized by its shrill quality in a mixed gathering of gulls and there is an angry *kik-kik-kik* when attacking intruders; but in winter the Common Gull is rather silent.

The nest may be sparsely lined or a substantial pad of stems, seaweed and debris, sited on rocks, shingle of beach or river, on moorland like a Lapwing, and on various artefacts and occasionally in trees. The clutch is of 2 or 3 eggs, pale blue or green to dark olive, blotched and spotted with dark brown and underlying grey. They are laid at about 48 hour intervals in a clutch of 3 and incubated from the last egg by both parents. The downy chicks, grey-brown with black streaks above, hatch in about $3\frac{1}{2}$ weeks and are tended by both parents, who sometimes attack and strike human intruders, but have to face the threat of foxes and rats, especially at the egg stage. The young fledge in about 5 weeks.

As inland breeding colonies were not counted, Operation Seafarer could not give an accurate estimate of the British and Irish breeding population in 1969-70; 12,400 pairs were reported, mostly in Scotland. But the Danish population in 1939 was estimated at half a million pairs, so that a Northern European total into 7 figures is likely.

Adult (below) and first winter bird (above)

Larus hyperboreus
GLAUCOUS GULL
LARIDAE 63·5 to 74 cm.

The two gulls considered on this page are both arctic in distribution and united by lack of black pigment on their wing-tips. Large Glaucous Gulls are bigger than a Great Black-back, white in summer except for the pale grey mantle, but with brown streaks on the head in winter. The juvenile is more or less uniform mottled dark and light brown all over, with a black-tipped flesh-coloured bill and pink legs; it appears much lighter than juvenile black-backs and Herring Gulls. The plumage becomes progressively paler each moult though maturity may not be attained for 4 or 5 years. The longer, heavier bill, massive head and relatively shorter wings are generally quoted as distinguishing the Glaucous from the Iceland Gull, but recent studies by S. Hedgren and L. Larsson and by R. A. Hume reveal many complications. The light yellow eye ring of the adult Glaucous, red on the Iceland, is about the one firm character.

Regarded as a northern counterpart of the Great Black-back, the Glaucous Gull has retreated before it in Iceland due, it is supposed, to climatic amelioration in the second quarter of the twentieth century. The 2 also overlap in north-west Russia but the Glaucous is unopposed in the arctic archipelago and breeds right round the northern coasts of Eurasia and America, seldom penetrating far inland. After breeding, the most northerly areas are deserted

gulls. Its behaviour resembles that of the Great Black-back, but in winter it seems to be more silent. The variety of breeding season calls is related to those of other gulls, and its displays follow the patterns described for the Herring Gull.

The Glaucous Gull breeds in colonies of up to 1000 pairs, on rocky coasts and islands. Where it overlaps with the Great Black-back, it nests higher up the rocks, to about 700 m. in Greenland, but it is not usually a cliff-ledge bird. The nest, built by both sexes, resembles that of other large gulls; laying starts in mid-May and the 2 or 3 eggs vary from light olive to buff with scrawls, spots, blotches in shades of dark brown and pale grey. They are laid at 2-day intervals and incubation, by both parents, begins with the first egg. The downy chicks, like Great Black-backs but with lighter streaking on the upper parts, hatch in about 4 weeks and are looked after by both parents.

Larus glaucoides
ICELAND GULL
LARIDAE 53 cm.

Named after a country in which it does not nest, the Iceland Gull has had its claims to specific status challenged. Some authorities see it as a link in the Herring and Lesser Black-backed Gull chain. In size it more or less agrees, but its plumage shows remarkable similarity to that of the Glaucous Gull at all ages and the writers

OPPOSITE *Glaucous Gulls, adult (below) and immature (above)*

BELOW *Iceland Gulls, adult (right) and immature (left)*

but there is no great shift southward, though immature birds may reach the Atlantic Islands. According to the severity of the winter, numbers vary along the North Sea coasts from Shetland to Norfolk in England.

Reports of the Glaucous Gull's predatory behaviour vary: reputed in Iceland to feed mainly on molluscs, crustaceans, dead fish and other shore carrion, it is regarded as the bane of the arctic seabird colonies, preying heavily on the Little Auk, and taking the eggs and young of other species. In winter it is a general scavenger, frequenting harbours as freely as other large

mentioned under that species suggest that size, wing length and other characters may not be reliable for identification; the position is further confused by albinistic and pale Herring Gulls and by hybrids between Glaucous and Herring Gulls, which are very common in Iceland. Hume suggests that the short bill of the Iceland Gull, not exceeding half the length of the head, and the more domed head shape are the best characters applying to all ages; the different-coloured eye ring only applies to the full adult breeding plumage.

The Iceland Gull's claim to be a North Euro-

pean breeding bird rests on the possibility of it nesting in Jan Mayen Island and occasionally in Iceland. Its main stronghold is southern Greenland and adjacent islands of arctic Canada; it favours high cliffs, up to 800 m., along the shores of fjords. The adults are largely sedentary but there is some occupation of northern Iceland in winter; immature birds move further south and are found in the North Sea area as well as the east coast of North America and the Great Lakes; these are just the birds that pose the identification problems.

The habits of the Iceland closely resemble those of the Herring Gull. It is credited with a faster beat of its relatively long wings, but this may be misleading unless both species are in the air together. It is said to be less predatory and to take more fish. Its voice is similar but shriller, with a loud, high-pitched greeting call and an *ack-ack-ack* of alarm (E. M. Nicholson). Iceland Gulls may breed in very large colonies, mixed with other species, either on cliffs or on rocky islands. A large nest of moss and grass is built and laying begins in late May. The 2 or 3 eggs are stone- or buff-coloured with dark brown markings.

Larus minutus
LITTLE GULL
LARIDAE 28 cm.

Included in the same genus as the larger white-headed gulls are a group of smaller species, of which this is the smallest, all showing in summer a dark chocolate to black hood and, in their actions and behaviour, some similarity to the terns. Adult Little Gulls are distinguished from the Black-headed Gull, easily the commonest member of the group in Northern Europe, by their more extensive and darker hoods, by the absence of black on the wings and by a dark slate grey underwing, light grey on the Black-headed. The last 2 characters are valid in winter when the hood is reduced to a dark spot behind the eye and the bill turns from red to blackish. The juvenile can be separated from the young Black-headed Gull by its dark crown and the inverted black W across the wings, recalling the Kittiwake's tarrock plumage; the back is heavily barred brown and the tail has a black terminal bar. The black areas are retained during the first full summer, though otherwise adult features appear; but the white underwing remains until the autumn moult in the second year and does not become dark for another year. Most birds start to breed in their third summer.

A tern-like feature of the Little Gull is its sporadic and capricious nesting, from Britain (first record 1975) across Eurasia, mainly between 50° and 60°N, the largest areas occupied being in west and east central Asia. In Northern

were reported on 23 estuaries in 1972–3 and up to 500 have been recorded on a loch in east Scotland.

In spite of its rather rounded wings, the Little Gull floats gracefully in the air like a tern, and swims buoyantly with head and tail raised like a paper boat. In summer it feeds largely on insects taken from the water in flight; in winter it fishes offshore, dipping just below the surface, and also takes crustaceans, molluscs and worms from the shore. The usual call is a rapid *kek kek kek*, similar to but softer than that of the Black-headed Gull. A higher-pitched *ka ka ka* is extended into the display call, often uttered in flight, when several birds may chase each other, the pursuer catching up with and gliding above the pursued, head raised and wings inclined downward; the roles may then be reversed (L. Tinbergen). On the ground there is a tern-like posture with head, bill and tail raised and wings lowered and depressed at the 'wrists'.

Little Gulls breed in colonies of up to 50 pairs, frequently with Black-headed Gulls and terns, in the tussocks surrounding a pool or among the emergent vegetation. The rather loose nest of stems and debris is built during courtship and laying usually begins in the second half of May with a 40-hour interval between the first and second, shorter between second and third eggs of the usual clutch. They are buff to olive-brown with dark brown and light grey markings. Incubation by both sexes begins with the first egg, which hatches in 3 to 3½ weeks, the chick enjoying preferential survival if food is short. The

OPPOSITE *Little Gulls, immature (top), summer adult (centre) and winter adult (below)*
BELOW *Mediterranean Gulls, summer adult (right) and winter (left)*

Europe there are colonies dotted about the North Sea and Baltic with a more solid zone inland to western Russia. Further south there are stations round the Black Sea, in the Caucasus and western Turkey. The breeding habitat is typically lush marshland with pools full of emergent water plants. Winter sees a complete change, the birds moving to large lakes, the coast and even the open sea but remaining in the temperate zone down to the Mediterranean. Some cross the Atlantic and a few pairs have bred in Ontario, Canada, since 1962. Britain and Ireland are mainly passage areas; Little Gulls

chicks have a thick down, dark greyish-buff above with small areas of blackish-brown. Cared for by both parents, they fly in 3 to 3¼ weeks.

Larus melanocephalus
MEDITERRANEAN GULL
LARIDAE 38·75 cm.

Although considered by K. H. Voous in 1960 to be a relict species on the way to extinction, the Mediterranean Gull has shown up increasingly in Northern Europe in recent years both in win-

ter and summer, perhaps because of greater skill in identifying it. Slightly larger and more imposing than the Black-headed Gull, the adult has a black and more extensive hood, a stouter red bill with a dusky band, and no black on the wing. Juvenile and immature birds show a rather close resemblance to Common Gulls of the same age, only analysed recently. 'Med. Gulls' become mature in their third year.

The main breeding area is round the Black and Aegean seas, with a curious enclave deep in central Asia. But from the 1930s single birds or pairs have appeared in Black-headed Gull colonies in the Baltic, the Netherlands and England, breeding true or hybridizing. Birds are also reported in winter, often from sewage outflows and frequently solitary among other species.

In habits the Mediterranean Gull closely resembles the Black-headed Gull, as far as is known, though the call note is much harsher. The nest-site and nest are also similar but the 2 to 3 eggs, laid from mid-May, often have a light ground with variable markings of dark brown and grey. The incubation and fledging periods appear to be unknown but the chicks have spiky down like that of some young terns.

Larus ridibundus
BLACK-HEADED GULL

LARIDAE 36 to 38 cm.

The most numerous and successful of the 'hooded' gulls of Northern Europe is familiar as a coastal, rural and urban bird. In spring the conspicuous chocolate mask is less extensive than the darker hoods of Little and Mediterranean Gulls; at all seasons the black-tipped wings and the narrow white band along the outer edge, contrasting with the grey upper surface, are good characters. The brown-capped juvenile has a mottled brown back and wing coverts and a dark brown bar near the end of the tail; bill and legs look dirty yellow in the field. Immature birds show more grey on the back in the first winter but retain some brown on the wings in their first full summer; they do not breed until their second summer. Like Common Gulls, Black-headed Gulls have brown eyes at all ages, but the head and neck are much more slender, the bill is red and a black spot is retained behind the eye after the mask is lost in late summer.

The Black-headed Gull is still confined to the Old World when breeding, but its increasing occurrence in North America suggests that it may be following its 'conquest' of Iceland since 1911. Eastward it nests in the Faeroe Islands and from Britain and Ireland right across Eurasia, mainly between 50° and 60°N. The habitat varies from coastal dunes and salt marshes and the shores and islands of rivers, lakes and lagoons, to moorland pools. After breeding there is a general shift southward and the British area receives birds from Iceland round to Poland; others reach the Mediterranean area and further south, but in general the species becomes more sedentary with age. There is also movement inland and to towns and ports: the Black-headed is the commonest gull in Reykjavik harbour in winter and, in Britain, where there has been a huge increase in the winter population inland this century, some 200,000 may roost on reservoirs in the London area alone.

Like the other hooded gulls, the Black-headed has a buoyant carriage on the water and a rather tern-like flight; it walks well without much waddle. Its feeding behaviour ranges from a raucous melee after offal, often competing with larger gulls, to following the plough in noisy flocks, 'pattering' on wet ground for worms, hawking after insects, from flying ants to large moths, robbing waterfowl on the water and Lapwings on land; it also takes fishes, though seldom by submerging. The variety of food taken is enormous and about a tenth of it is vegetable.

Feeding is accompanied by harsh calls from a staccato *kek* to a hoarse drawn-out cawing, given with open beak and sometimes polysyllabic: it appears to have several functions. A bedlam of calls issues from a large colony, apparently for all 24 hours of a summer day. The behaviour of the Black-headed Gull was a pioneer study by F. B. Kirkman, followed up by N. Tinbergen and his colleagues. As with other gulls, a considerable effort is needed to overcome mutual antagonism before the pair forms; head-flagging, in which the innocuous white nape is presented to the partner, is an important component of the appeasing routine; the mask carries with it the element of hostility.

Breeding is usually highly colonial, though solitary nests are found, and may involve thousands of pairs scattered over *Spartina* grass, sand dunes or wet moors. Colonies of terns often form alongside and ducks and grebes may incubate apparently safely among the gulls. The nest, built by both sexes of local plant stems, may float in water, rest on aquatic plants, or be little more than a scrape on dry ground; tree nests are not unknown. Laying begins early in April and both parents share incubation from the first egg. The usual clutch is 3 eggs, of blue, green or brown ground, with dark brown and grey markings. The downy young, dark buff streaked with black above, light buff below, hatch in 22 to 24 days and fly in 5 or 6 weeks, after attention from both parents. J. J. M. Flegg and C. J. Cox have shown that the heaviest adult mortality at an English (Kentish) colony is during the breeding season.

Since Operation Seafarer did not include inland stations, no comprehensive estimate exists for the total breeding population of Britain and Ireland; at a guess it may be about 250,000 pairs. In 1969–70 some 74,500 pairs nested coastally: the colony at Needs Oar Point, Hampshire, held about 15,000.

OPPOSITE *Black-headed Gulls, immature (left) adult in winter plumage (centre) and summer adult (right)*
ABOVE *Sabine's Gulls, immature (above) and summer adult (below)*

Larus sabini

SABINE'S GULL

LARIDAE 33 cm.

This far northern breeding species is distinguished by its forked tail and by a wing pattern of 3 triangles: grey (upper coverts), black (outer primaries) and white (trailing edge). In summer the adult has an extensive, black-fringed, grey hood. The eye is brown, eye-ring red, legs black and bill grey with a yellow tip. The juvenile, most likely to be seen, has a grey-brown crown and upper parts and black band on the tail. First-winter birds show a mixture of adult and juvenile plumage. Sabine's Gull breeds in Svalbard and in parts of arctic Asia and North America; it is most often seen in Northern Europe in autumn and winter. It feeds off the water in graceful, tern-like flight and its usual harsh call is also tern-like. It nests on the tundra, laying 3 eggs, darker than those of most gulls, at the end of June. Incubated by both parents, they hatch in 23 to 26 days; the downy young are brown-buff above, paler below.

131

Rissa tridactyla
KITTIWAKE
LARIDAE 41 cm.

This is another successful species, though its oceanic way of life differs considerably from that of the shore-haunting *Larus* gulls. Most likely to be confused with the Common Gull, the Kittiwake has a neat black triangular tip to its darker wing, with no white 'mirror' beyond, and its short, 3-toed feet are black. The yellow bill opens to reveal a striking orange gape. In winter the adult's crown and nape have a greyish tinge. The juvenile or 'tarrock' is curiously like the juvenile Little Gull, with an open black W right across the wings, a black bar near the end of the slightly forked tail and a dark spot behind the eye. It also has a black band at the nape; this, however, disappears by the first summer and at 2 years old the plumage is virtually adult, though breeding usually begins at 3 years old.

The Kittiwake has a widespread breeding range along the cliff-bound coasts of the northern hemisphere, to over 80°N in the New Siberian Islands and below 50°N in the Kurile Islands (part of the range of the Pacific race *pollicaris*). The Northern European distribution covers the island groups from Iceland to Franz Josef Land and Novaya Zemlya, the northern coast of Scandinavia, the Faeroe Islands, Britain, Ireland, the Channel Islands, Brittany and Denmark, where it nests on flat, rocky Hirsholm in the Kattegat. There are also one or two beach colonies, but this is typically a bird of the sea cliffs, sharing them with the auks. After breeding, there is a wide dispersal and many European birds cross the Atlantic or spend the winter over its northern waters. Others move south to visit the Mediterranean and North African coasts.

Another difference from the Common Gull is the Kittiwake's faster wing-beat and generally swifter flight. Although usually seen on the wing, it may land on the sea and in summer birds stream to and from fresh waters where they bathe and preen; in autumn flocks, often largely of tarrocks, rest on flat shores with terns. Kittiwakes feed by picking off the water in flight, diving from the surface or by plunging with open wings: this method is used when fishing and when offal-hunting behind ships. During the breeding season sand eels and other small fish are the main prey but many small animals of the plankton are eaten, and insects taken in flight.

Away from the breeding colonies, Kittiwakes tend to be silent but may call in excitement when attacking a shoal of fish. The best-known call is the loud onomatopoeic *kitti-wa-a-k*, associated with displays at the nest-site, when the members of a pair face each other, calling and making a variety of head movements; they also 'gulp', bow and sometimes open their wings. Mated birds rub bills and mating usually takes place at the nest. Squabbles with intruders also take place at this precarious focus, the gestures used looking similar to those of courtship.

Towards the south of their range Kittiwakes may visit the colonial breeding cliffs from January to November, roosting at sea and occupying them again at dawn; in the Arctic this is impossible before March. As well as cliffs, buildings close to the sea are being increasingly colonized, especially in Norway and along the British coast, where some Kittiwakes nest 15 km. up the estuary of the Tyne. A windowsill makes a very suitable artefact equivalent to the natural protuberances on which the pair manages to fasten the bracket nest with its foundation of green algae and excrement, covered with debris and mud and a final cup of grass. The normal clutch is of 2 eggs, pale grey to light brown with dark brown and grey markings, laid from early May and incubated by both parents. The young, which have plain grey down, hatch in 3 to 3½ weeks and cling to the nest while the parents feed them for up to 6 weeks. They do not leave until well able to fly and may occasionally return to be fed. Operation Seafarer estimated the 1969–70 population at about 470,000 pairs in Britain and Ireland (of which over three-quarters were round the Scottish coasts), making it the most numerous gull.

Pagophila eburnea
IVORY GULL
LARIDAE 44·5 cm.

The more northerly the range, the whiter the plumage seems to be the rule with gulls. This beautiful arctic bird is pure white when adult, with black legs, grey to yellow, red-tipped bill, and red-ringed brown eyes. Immatures have some grey markings, with black spots on the upper parts, black tips to primary feathers and tail, and brown eye-ring. The breeding range is discontinuous from arctic Canada to Greenland, Svalbard, Franz Josef Land, northern Novaya Zemlya and the New Siberian Islands. Ivory Gulls winter on the edge of the pack-ice but occasionally wander further south; there are about 80 British records. They are scavengers, but also take marine crustaceans, and chironomid larvae when breeding. P. P. G. Bateson and R. C. Plowright described the display on Svalbard as containing movements similar to those of other gulls: 'choking', 'head-tossing' and 'head-flagging', the oblique and long calls. The usual flight call is 'harsh and discordant' (F. C. R. Jourdain). Colonies of up to 500 pairs occur, sometimes on cliffs with other seabirds, sometimes on islands safe from arctic foxes. The 2 olive to olive-buff eggs, heavily marked in darker shades, are laid from late June. The young hatch in grey down with white tips; both parents tend them.

*Adult Kittiwake (below) and tarrock
or immature (above)*

Sterna hirundo
COMMON TERN

LARIDAE 33 to 36 cm. (varying with length of tail-streamers).

Terns, poetically sea-swallows, show few hirundine characters except their forked tails and narrow pointed wings but have a grace all their own which picks them out from the sturdy utilitarian gulls. The Common and Arctic Terns are traditionally difficult to separate, but recently J. R. Jacobsen and several British ornithologists have elucidated new points of difference, summarized here, together with standard information, to show how much can still be discovered about the plumages of quite common birds.

The Common Tern is slightly larger than the Arctic, has a longer, somewhat stouter bill, longer legs, shorter tail-streamers and paler under parts, all characters of reduced value if no field comparisons can be made. In summer the Common Tern's coral-red bill with black tip is distinctive, though some Arctics show darker tips to their blood-red bills; in winter the Common's legs become reddish-brown, the Arctic's legs become black. In 1953 R. A. Richardson pointed out that, viewed from below, against the light, all the flight feathers of the Arctic Tern are translucent (except the tips of the primaries), against only the inner primaries of the Common Tern. Then in 1961 Jacobsen noted that, from above, the outer 5 to 7 primaries of the Common Tern's wing look much darker than the rest of the flight feathers, while on the innermost of these dark feathers there is often a noticeable darker wedge, pointing forwards. In good light, according to R. A. Hume and P. J. Grant, this feature can be seen up to 1 km. away. Not all birds show it and its absence does not necessarily identify a bird as an Arctic Tern.

The discrimination of juvenile plumages is also difficult, but Grant and R. E. Scott point out that the more heavily built Common Tern shows a gingery brown wash, usually lost by late autumn, over forehead and mantle. Other distinctions of the Common juvenile are the opaqueness of the primaries from below, a dark trailing edge to the underwing and a blackish bar at the carpal joint, which shows up well when the wing is folded; the smaller dark area on the Arctic juvenile is almost hidden in this position. The Common Tern's rump is pale grey, but pure white on Arctic and Roseate juveniles. The Common's legs are orange, those of the Arctic usually redder; the bills of both juveniles are blackish with some pink (Common) or dark red (Arctic) at the base. Adults of both species have white foreheads in winter and black bills, the Common Tern retaining some red at the base. Immature plumages resemble winter adults; their persistence into summer, even on breeding birds, led at one time to suggestions of an 'S. portlandica'.

As a breeding bird the Common Tern occupies much of the northern hemisphere, mainly inland, though in Britain and Scandinavia it is primarily coastal. The range stretches right across Eurasia, mostly between 40° and 60°N, to Kamtchatka and the Kurile Islands. There are colonies on the Atlantic islands off North Africa and one as far south as the mouth of the Niger. In North America Common Terns breed over a large part of Canada south-west from Hudson Bay and sporadically down the east coast, crossing the Caribbean to islands off Venezuela. The habitat varies from rocky islands and sandy beaches to lake margins and riparian shingle, moorland, and steppes up to 4600 m. in Tibet. Most terns are highly migratory; this species moves south to the subtropics and tropics, reaching Patagonia, South Africa and north-west Australia.

OPPOSITE *Summer adult with chick*
ABOVE *Head of adult in winter*

The Common Tern's flight appears languid and halting, the pronounced wing-beats lifting the body and jerking it from side to side; but at times the action can be more purposeful. When feeding, the bird flies some feet above the water, bill angled downwards, then, after perhaps a short hover, plunges just below the surface, the half-closed wings usually remaining clear. Much of the diet is small fish, especially sand eels, but crustaceans, molluscs, marine worms, echinoderms and, over land, some insects are also taken. In times of shortage Common Terns rob each other of fish (E. K. Dunn). They generally swim only when bathing but roosting on water inland has recently been reported by J. C. Rolls. They perch freely on the shore and on buoys and posts, but walk awkwardly. The most frequently heard calls are the harsh *kee-raah*, distinguishable with practice from the similar note of the Arctic Tern, and a rapid *kek kek kek* uttered in various contexts and extended into an excited *keeri keeri*. The male growls *korrr korrr* when flying in with fish to present to his mate. The 'fish flight' is the most prominent of many display actions, which include aerial chases and glides. The mass 'dread' is described under the next species.

The exposed nest may be a bare scrape on a rock or lined by both sexes with local plant stems, marram grass on dunes, for example; sometimes it forms a substantial floating pad.

The 2 to 4 pale green, blue, cream or brown eggs, often boldly marked with dark brown and grey, are laid from mid-May in Northern Europe and incubated by both parents. The downy young, buff streaked with black above, with a black throat and white under parts, hatch in 22 to 26 days, are fed by both parents and fly in about 4 weeks, then collect in parties before migrating. Population figures for Britain and Ireland are available from 1969 until 1974, when the total was about 10,000 pairs (C. S. Lloyd, C. J. Bibby and M. J. Everett).

Sterna paradisaea
ARCTIC TERN
LARIDAE 36 to 38 cm.

Despite its apparently casual flight and slender form, this is one of the world's greatest travellers: a juvenile from Anglesey (Wales) reached New South Wales within 6 months, a minimum journey of 20,000 km. (R. Spencer). The Arctic Tern's pectorals are said to be the most efficient voluntary muscles in the animal kingdom. Many points of difference from the Common Tern have been pointed out under that species. In addition the Arctic has a characteristic short-necked silhouette; due to the rather small, rounded head and the long tail-streamers, the wings appear to be set further forward on the body than on the Common Tern. At fairly close quarters and in good light the dark or blood-red bill is distinctive, even without a Common Tern for comparison. The chick may be either grey or brown, each form predominating against the corresponding background colour; in general it looks similar to Common chicks but has heavier black markings above and the dark throat colour extends to the chin and forehead.

A map of their breeding distributions shows that this species is the northern replacer of the Common Tern; their main overlap is in Northern Europe: in Britain, Ireland, Brittany, the North Sea and Baltic coasts and northern Scandinavia. The Arctic Tern also breeds in the arctic archipelagos, Iceland, the Faeroe Islands and north-western Russia, whence it extends in some depth along the Siberian seaboard, over much of Alaska, arctic Canada and coastal Greenland, overlapping with the Common Tern again in New England. The habitat is generally tundra or rocky skerries. After breeding, their great migration takes many Arctic Terns into the long daylight of the Antarctic, where they meet the relatively sedentary Antarctic Tern, *S. vittata*, considered to be an offshoot in fairly recent times. Northern European birds travel down the west coasts of Europe and Africa, joined by North American birds from across the Atlantic; from South Africa they cross south-east towards the pack-ice, odd birds reaching nearly 80°S. Immature birds may stay south for their first summer or longer; breeding usually begins at 3 years old.

The Arctic Tern's food varies with latitude. In Svalbard, many small crustaceans are taken; in Novaya Zemlya, small fish and large insects; in arctic Canada adults feed on amphipods and small squids, giving their chicks small fish; in Iceland flies are hawked off lake surfaces, while Farne Islands (Northumbrian) birds catch sand eels, sprats and other small fish with some crustaceans and squids (various sources summarized by D. R. Saunders). Occasionally they follow the plough like gulls. Round the Farnes, Common Terns fish mainly just offshore, Arctic Terns out to sea, but their methods are much the same. In general the habits of the 2 species are similar and so are some of their calls. But, in the *kee-raah*, the Arctic emphasizes the second syllable, or may shorten it to a single harsh *kaah*. There is also a distinctive trisyllabic greeting call.

The displays of the Common and Arctic Terns will always be associated with the pioneer research of G. and A. Marples. Fish-carrying and presentation are important in Arctic as well as Common Tern behaviour; there are also high flights, similar to those of the Roseate Tern (J. M. Cullen). Head and neck movements occur in greeting but the body is stretched forward in territorial squabbles. The Marples first named the colonial 'dread', in which, after a rise in the volume of noise, there is a sudden pause before most or all of the birds sweep silently out over the sea, returning a few minutes later to resume normal activity. Dreads take place among other social nesting species as well as terns, probably as a predator reaction.

The male initiates the nest scrape, though his mate may prefer her own: it is usually sparsely lined with local plant stems, debris or pebbles and may be exposed or well hidden. The one to 3 eggs, laid from mid-May in Northern Europe, cannot be told from Common Terns'. They hatch after about 3 weeks incubation by the parents, and the chicks are fed about 25 times a day each (T. H. Pearson), fledging in 3 or 4 weeks. The Arctic is the most aggressive of the terns when breeding, concerting attacks on intruders (E. K. Dunn). Some 28,000 pairs bred at

OPPOSITE *Adult Arctic Terns, summer (bottom) and winter (centre). Caspian Tern adult in summer (top)*
BELOW *Head of Arctic Tern adult in winter*

main sites in Britain and Ireland in 1974; the full total may well be about 50,000. The Finnish total has been estimated as 6000 and the German at 1000 pairs. Pairs may nest singly as well as colonially.

Hydroprogne caspia syn. *Sterna caspia*
CASPIAN TERN
LARIDAE 48 to 56 cm.

The largest tern, patterned like its smaller relatives, is about the size of a Herring Gull; the

black crown extends just below the eye, the strong red bill is prominent; the wings and mantle are grey, the tips dark grey above, blackish below; the under parts and slightly forked tail are white, the legs black. In winter the crown is flecked white, there is a dark patch below the eye and the bill becomes duller. The juvenile has a mottled black and grey back, the crown and bill much as the winter adult. The mapped breeding distribution of the Caspian Tern looks like a world-wide outbreak of measles: there are spots in all continents except South America, with a larger area east of the Caspian Sea. In Northern Europe it nests on islands in the inner Baltic, a population estimated in 1950 at about 1200 pairs. These are believed to winter in the tropics. In spite of its size the Caspian Tern flies as gracefully as its relatives, sometimes soaring, and plunges after fish, its chief diet. The usual calls are a deep caw and a repeated *kuk*. The Baltic colonies are from single to tens of pairs. The large scrape holds 2 or 3 stone-buff, sparsely overmarked eggs, which are laid in June and incubated by both parents for 20 to 22 days. The buffish-grey chicks, spotted on their upper parts and white below, fly at about 4 weeks old.

Sterna dougallii
ROSEATE TERN

LARIDAE 36 to 38 cm. (including outer tail feathers: 20 cm.)

On 12 July 1812, Dr MacDougall of Glasgow and some friends landed on a small island in Millport Bay, Great Cumbrae, where there was a large colony of terns. Certain birds, distinguished by whiteness of plumage and by the elegance of motion were 'easily singled out by the sportsmen' and dispatched. The victims of this minor holocaust were seen in the hand to have a rosy suffusion of the breast and the doctor secured immortality by sending one to Colonel George Montagu, who named the new species after him.

In fact the tint which gives the English name and looks so attractive in illustrations is not conspicuous in the field. Several other terns and gulls show it, but not to the extent that it colours the flamingoes. The suffusion is believed to be chemical in origin, derived from the diet of small marine or brackish water animals. Certainly it disappears when the birds are ill or deprived of their natural food.

The elegance which impressed Dr MacDougall is due to the long tail streamers and to the shallow wing-beats, faster than those of the Common and Arctic Terns, from which the apparently dead white breast is a good field distinction, though it is shared by the larger Sandwich Tern.

but much fragmented breeding range, complicated by continual fluctuations in the size and location of the colonies. At present the British and Irish colonies appear, apart from some in Brittany, to be the only ones in Europe. Elsewhere groups are found in eastern North America, the Caribbean and the Azores; along the Red Sea and East African coasts, on various islands in the Indian Ocean across to Indonesia, the Ryu Kyus and on to Australasia.

While Roseates are resident in some parts of this complex distribution, European birds have a regular migration which takes them to winter along the West African coast between the equator and 10°N. First year birds stay in the south; some 2-year-olds return north in spring, but apparently most European Roseates do not breed until their third summer, arriving from late April onwards, but not much in evidence except at the breeding stations, where their variously described guttural alarm note *aach* and the softer *chevick* when carrying fish stand out from the *kee-rah* of Common and Arctic Terns. Many other notes have been recorded during displays, which resemble those of their near relatives. But J. M. Cullen found them 'more mercurial' than Arctics and also subject to 'dreads'. As well as ground displays with presentation of fish and mutual 'nibbling' after mating, Cullen described the high flight, when 2 birds rise in spirals with wings angled back and beating

OPPOSITE *Adult Roseate Terns in summer (bottom and centre) and in winter (top)*
BELOW *Juvenile Roseate Tern*

At close range the almost black, red-based bill is a good character. The black cap of summer recedes in winter (shown opposite in background) and the legs become brownish-red. The juvenile (shown on this page) has mottled black and grey upper parts, black legs and black bill. The nestling, sandy-buff striped black above and white below, shares with the Sandwich Tern chick the 'spiky' or 'hairy' appearance due to groups of downy filaments being held together at their tips by a common sheath. Its legs and bill are varying shades of grey.

The Roseate Tern has an almost cosmopolitan

faster than normally; this is followed by swift descent, one bird overtaking the other.

Roseates hunt on the wing, taking small fish like sprats and sand eels from the surface, but E. K. Dunn found that in some places they regularly rob other terns and sometimes their own species of prey which they are bringing back to their nestlings.

Usually nesting in discrete groups among or on the edge of aggregations of other terns, Roseates occasionally form mixed pairs with one of their neighbours. Their breeding habitat varies from low rocky, sandy or grassy islets to beaches

of sand and shingle, always by the sea in Europe. The actual site is often well hidden in dense vegetation, even rabbit burrows. A Roseate in good plumage perched on a flowering tree mallow above its nest makes a memorable picture. But sometimes open scrapes are used, seldom with any lining. Laying in Northern Europe begins at the end of May and clutches are of one or 2 eggs; a genuine 3 is exceptional. The rather elongated egg is cream or buff, with brown freckles and streaks and fainter ashy marks. Both parents share incubation for 21 to 26 days and feed the young, which fledge in 3 to 4 weeks,

but leave the nest much sooner.

Operation Seafarer found that in 1969–70 the breeding population in Britain and Ireland was 2367 pairs, of which nearly three-quarters were in Ireland. To what extent there has been a decrease after a build-up in the first half of the century it is hard to say, owing to the violent, often annual, fluctuations between the colonies.

The 1974 total for the 12 main sites was only 1414 pairs. Although this is slightly better than the figures for 1972 and 1973, the Roseate Tern's status in Northern Europe is obviously precarious.

Sterna albifrons
LITTLE TERN
LARIDAE 23 to 25 cm.

The future of the smallest European tern, despite its widespread distribution, is causing considerable anxiety to conservationists in areas, such as Britain, Belgium and the Netherlands, where it breeds mainly on coastal beaches that have been increasingly overrun by holiday-making humanity. Somehow, in spite of its ability to make long migrations, the Least Tern, as it is called in America, looks frail and in need of help. Its dark-tipped pale grey wings, mantle and rump, white under parts and forked tail conform with its relatives, but its forehead remains white in all plumages, a black stripe running from the crown through the eye to the base of the yellow, black-tipped bill; the legs are also yellow. In winter the white forehead area is more extensive and the crown becomes ashy-grey, tinged with brown. The juvenile is generally white below and ashy-grey above with a sandy-buff suffusion of the forehead, dark-streaked crown and upper back, on which there are prominent dark brown 'horseshoes' – subterminal marks on individual feathers. The primaries are darker than on the adult and the inner tail feathers have dark sub-terminal patches. The legs and bill are brownish yellow. By the first winter the plumage is nearer the adult, but the tail feathers, primaries and dark-shafted secondaries remain from the juvenile phase. By the first summer the Little Tern's appearance is virtually adult. At a distance, juveniles of other terns, due to their whitish foreheads and shortish wings, can be mistaken for Little Terns, which are, however, much smaller and have narrower wings.

Whereas the Roseate Tern has a purely coastal breeding distribution in 5 continents, the Little Tern extends inland in much the same latitudes, roughly between 60°N and the equator, though reaching nearly 40°S down the west side of Australia. It is found right round the European coastline, except for northern Scandinavia; eastward and inland it reaches far into central Asia. The Northern European range includes Britain, except Orkney and Shetland, and Ireland, the Channel and North Sea coasts (though now lost to Belgium), Denmark and extreme south Sweden with the islands of Öland and Gotland. Its preferred European habitat is a sand, shingle, shell or even muddy beach, either by the sea, a lagoon or lake, or on similar beaches and beds along rivers; in the tropics lowlying rocky coasts and coral reefs are occupied. These are also among the winter homes of the northern breeding population. Juveniles are on the move in August; one ringed at Bradwell, Essex, in 1966 was recovered not more than a week later in Portugal, having travelled about 1600 km. by the shortest sea

route (R. Spencer). But some movements, even in Britain where the breeding distribution is coastal, are inland.

Little Terns fish in the general neighbourhood of their colonies, at which (in Northern Europe) they arrive in April and early May; they are often first seen as they hover with rapidly fluttering wings and depressed tail over shallow water, to plunge, rising almost at once if unsuccessful, and resume their search, after flying onwards a few yards. Their diet seems to vary from one almost entirely of small fish, especially sand eels, to one of crustaceans and marine worms, probably caught on the ebb tide. The high-pitched *kik kik kik* call may be heard from foraging birds and is used in several situations. Over the breeding grounds the excited *kirri kirri* may signal one of the aerial display flights, which are distinguished by a slow-beating action, or by sailing along with wings held in a V (G. and A. Marples). Sometimes the birds attain a great height, then descend rapidly. As with other terns, the presentation of fish is an important element in pair-forming.

Although normally colonial, Little Terns, at least in Northern Europe, tend to nest in groups of 10 to 20 pairs rather than in the large aggregations favoured by their relatives. Both sexes play a part in scrape-forming in the sand or mud, the chosen hollow being usually unadorned, though small pebbles may be selected as a lining on shingle beaches. No use is made of cover and several nests may lie along the same contour of the beach. The 2 or 3 eggs, stone-coloured, light green or blue, with rather fine brown spots and prominent ashy-grey markings, are laid from the second week of May in southern Britain. Both birds share the incubation, usually from the second egg, and the chicks hatch in 19 to 22 days. They are clad in rather short, hair-like down, sandy on the crown and upper parts, mottled and streaked with dark brown, the under parts white or pale buff. They leave the scrape after about a day and are tended by both parents, flying first after less than 3 weeks.

The Little Tern seems to be declining over much of its wide range. Operation Seafarer put the British and Irish breeding population in 1969–70 at 1814 pairs in 168 colonies, almost all coastal and often close to high water mark. Nests, in fact, are quite often washed away and this, with other weather hazards and human disturbance, adds to the difficulties facing the species. On the other hand, in Norfolk and elsewhere, several pairs of Ringed Plovers may nest among a group of Little Terns, apparently for protection: the terns certainly buzz human intruders bravely if ineffectively. Attempts are now being made to induce them to nest at safer sites a little way inland, for example on artificial islands in man-made pools as at the RSPB's reserve at Minsmere in Suffolk.

Immature (top left) and two summer adults

Sterna sandvicensis
SANDWICH TERN
LARIDAE 38 to 43 cm.

All terns are somewhat capricious over their breeding sites, none more so than this species, named in 1787 by J. Latham after a Kentish locality whence it has long vanished. Its stouter body with relatively short forked tail gives it a less graceful appearance than its relatives; it looks as white as a Roseate Tern in flight and also shows briefly a pink suffusion on the under parts. The yellow-tipped black bill, shaggy crest and black legs combine to make the summer adult unmistakable at reasonable range. The crown often begins to show white flecks during the summer and the forehead turns white. The juvenile's freckled crown looks brownish in the field and the back is mottled buff and black at first, becoming paler by the first winter when it is very like an adult, except for some bronzy marks on the wings, and black outer tail webs.

The breeding distribution of the Sandwich Tern is fragmented but less extensive than the Caspian Tern's, being confined to both sides of the Atlantic. The most stable area is, in fact, Northern Europe, with colonies in Britain (including Orkney, the most northerly in the world), Ireland, Brittany, the Netherlands, Germany, Denmark and south Sweden. Other Old World stations are by the Black and Caspian seas and in Tunisia. The transatlantic race *acuflavida*, Cabot's Tern, is found mostly round the Caribbean and K. H. Voous includes with it the yellow-billed Cayenne Tern, *S. eurygnatha*. The most favoured breeding habitats are sand dunes and low rocky islets adjacent to clear water for fishing. Dispersal of juveniles precedes migration southward from the North European breeding area, which is deserted by October. The main wintering area is off the West African coast from Senegal to Ghana and Angola, but some birds round the Cape of Good Hope and reach Natal. Birds from the Black Sea winter in the Mediterranean where immature North European birds may spend the summer, though the majority seem to stay further south. Some 2-year-olds return north and breed, though this is not general until the third summer (H. W. Nehls, A. J. M. Smith).

The far-carrying *kirrick* call is often the first evidence of Sandwich Terns as they fly offshore between their fishing grounds and the colony. They fish by plunging from a height on a slant, submerging sometimes for several seconds; hovering may precede the plunge. The food is predominantly fish, in summer mainly sand eels and sprats. Fish-carrying and presentation form part of the display; more dramatic are the high flights of 2 to 4 birds, which ascend almost out of sight, then glide down with dazzling manoeuvres, calling as they come. Although pairs often form before arrival at the colony, greeting ceremonies continue to cement the bond. Display brings forth a number of 'low, guttural or croaking sounds' (G. and A. Marples); there is a special brooding call, and a harsh note when attacking an intruder.

From long experience at Scolt Head (Norfolk, England), R. Chestney believes that a small vanguard, arriving in April, establishes the site each season, the bulk of the birds settling round them. If the early birds are disturbed or the weather is bad, the colony may not form and the latecomers go elsewhere. The groups forming a large colony lay with remarkable synchronization (Smith). The nests, sometimes less than a metre apart, are usually almost bare scrapes made by both sexes and receive one or 2 whitish, cream or light brown eggs with a variety of reddish-brown spots and smears and prominent grey markings. Both parents incubate them from the first egg, laid from late April onwards. The young, variable but generally with light spiky down like Roseate Terns, hatch in 3 to 4 weeks and fledge in about 4 weeks, but may remain in some sort of parental care for perhaps 4 months; and their fishing ability matures in 7 to 9 months (E. K. Dunn). Sandwich Terns often nest near Black-headed Gull colonies, apparently deriving some protection from them. The colonial nuclei become shining white with accumulation of faeces. Ringing has shown that birds move between colonies in Northern Europe, which might be expected owing to their somewhat ephemeral character. The 1974 breeding population in Britain and Ireland was over 12,000 pairs, out of an estimated North European total of some 30,000 pairs.

Geochelidon nilotica
GULL-BILLED TERN
LARIDAE 36 to 38 cm.

Superficially resembling the Sandwich Tern, this is a longer-legged, shorter-bodied species with a less forked tail and a powerful all-black bill with a marked gonys or angle on the lower mandible; the legs are black. In winter the head turns whitish grey. The juvenile resembles the winter adult but has a buffish tinge to the crown and upper parts and brown mottling on the back; its legs are reddish-brown. This is largely an inland breeding tern, though also found on saline lagoons and sandy shores. Its North European foothold is precarious, in Denmark and in Schleswig-Holstein, where nesting was reported in 1975. There are a number of scattered stations in southern Europe and a more continuous area from the Balkans and Asia Minor into central Asia; the other main centres of distribution are Central America and south-western Australia. European birds probably winter by the East African lakes.

Unlike the other terns described, Gull-billed Terns hunt largely over land for invertebrates

and small vertebratęs; they also fish in tidal and
fresh waters. Their displays include aerial evolutions. The breeding colonies vary in size and
consist of nest scrapes on sand or grass. The 2
or 3 eggs, laid from the end of May in Denmark,
are yellowish, cream or brown, sparingly marked
with sepia; both parents incubate them for over
3 weeks. The downy chicks are grey-buff above,
streaked with black, white below. They begin to
fly after about 4 weeks.

*Sandwich Terns, adult in summer (foreground) and
first winter bird (behind)*

143

Alca torda
RAZORBILL
ALCIDAE 41 cm. (25 cm. high).

The auks are called the penguins of the northern hemisphere, but the similarity is one of convergence and, except for the extinct Great Auk, *Pinguinus impennis*, the species existing in historic times, have retained the power of flight. The general livery, dark upper and white under parts, is penguin-like; the plumages of the sexes are alike throughout the family.

The adult Razorbill (left opposite) is one of the darkest auks when in summer plumage. Stouter than the guillemots, it also looks more buoyant on the water, where the pointed tail is often raised when swimming. The white line across the vertically compressed bill and up to the eye is distinctive in summer but less obvious in winter plumage. The juvenile has a dark brown head and neck; first winter birds have a smaller, unmarked bill which can cause confusion with northern races of the Guillemot.

Two races of Razorbill, indistinguishable in the field, are endemic to the North Atlantic and breed round both the Baltic and open coasts of Scandinavia, the British Isles, the Faeroe Islands, Iceland, west Greenland and on the east coast of North America. The outlying colony on Lake Ladoga is the only known auk breeding place on an inland water. In winter Razorbills move out to sea and further south, entering the Mediterranean.

Razorbills may be seen standing or squatting on the rocks near their breeding places, swimming or flying low over the sea, sometimes in long lines. They flirt legs and wings when diving but apparently only use the wings under water, travelling faster than on the surface in pursuit of crustaceans and small fish, down to 7·6 m. But a minute's dive is exceptional. They also take molluscs and annelid worms. Display is largely mutual; partners nibble each other's head and neck feathers and 'kiss' with their bills. Mating takes place on land. On the water there are excited communal splashings and more formalized movements. The usual call is a grating *karrr*. The single large, variable egg is laid from early May onwards on rock or earth in a crevice, under a boulder or on an open ledge like a Guillemot; both parents incubate it for about 4 weeks. After about a fortnight they encourage the chick to flutter down to sea, where both feed it at first. The precise fledging period is hard to determine.

Operation Seafarer estimated the total British and Irish breeding population in 1969–70 as at least 144,000 pairs. There had been no previous survey, but some evidence for recent decreases in the southern part of the British area and in north and west Scotland. However there are indications of increases at several colonies where Guillemots appear to have decreased.

Uria aalge
COMMON GUILLEMOT
ALCIDAE 42 cm. (25 cm. high).

Guillemots (bottom right opposite) are generally more numerous than Razorbills at their communal colonies. The southern race *albionis*, nesting up to southern Scotland, has chocolate upper parts; the northern races, *aalge* and *hyperborea*, are almost as dark as Razorbills. The black bill (which has a yellow gape) is straight and pointed, the legs mostly yellowish and the eyes very dark brown. The conspicuous bridled variety is shown far left in the group. Juveniles have blackish margins to the feathers of the back, but by their first winter closely resemble adults.

The Guillemot's North Atlantic breeding distribution resembles the Razorbill's, except that it is scarcer in the Baltic but extends to northwest Iberia; it has a second range on both sides of the North Pacific. In winter birds disperse out to sea, generally within the latitudes of the breeding range.

Guillemots crowded from April onwards on their breeding ledges are the layman's idea of a seabird; their beautifully variegated eggs, once taken for food, became tourist trophies until protected by law. The Guillemot's general behaviour is much like the Razorbill's, but it dives deeper and longer, over half the diet being small fish. There is much bill play in Guillemot displays, but more communal activity than among Razorbills and a greater variety of harsh calls, probably due to the much larger and congested colonies. Mating takes place on land and laying begins in mid-May in the south. The single egg is pear-shaped, adapted not to roll off the bare ledge. The parents share incubation for about 4 weeks, and the young one descends to the sea after about a fortnight, to be tended at first by both adults. The estimated British and Irish breeding population in 1969–70 was nearly 577,000 pairs, four-fifths of them in Scotland; there is evidence of decreases in the southern range and in western Scotland, though these may be balanced by increases elsewhere.

Uria lomvia
BRÜNNICH'S GUILLEMOT
ALCIDAE 42 cm.

This species replaces the Guillemot in the far north, nesting abundantly in Iceland and the arctic archipelagos. Its upper parts are very dark, but its distinguishing features are the rather stouter bill with fairly pronounced gonys and a pale line along the 'cutting edge' of the upper mandible. In other respects the 2 species are remarkably similar.

*Three Razorbills in summer (left). Common Guillemots
in summer (centre) and bridled form (far right)*

145

Cepphus grylle
BLACK GUILLEMOT
ALCIDAE 34 cm.

Unlike its larger relatives in eschewing the more exposed cliff-bound coasts and in laying more than a single egg, the Black Guillemot, often called by its Nordic name Tystie, is in summer unlike all other North European seabirds in its combination of stoutish body·and black-brown plumage, uniform except for a broad white patch on the wing. The legs and gape are bright red. During the moult, which in a whole population may continue from July to December, the birds look 'odd and patchy' (B. W. Tucker); in full winter plumage the broad wing bar remains white, the head and under parts become mainly white, but the upper parts, including wings and tail, are barred with black and white and the sides of the head are similarly mottled. Juveniles look much darker, with blackish backs and sooty-brown mottlings which obscure the wing patch. By their first winter they are much more like adults, but retain the juvenile wing pattern. In all these plumages, which look greyish-white at a distance, some confusion with winter grebes and other guillemots is possible.

K. H. Voous considers that species formation through geographical isolation is at work 'in the group of Black Guillemots', but continues to regard them as one, though suggesting that the North-east Pacific form *carbo* should be given specific status. Most authorities also separate the Pacific Pigeon Guillemot as *C. columba*, confining *C. grylle* to east North America and Greenland, the arctic archipelagos, Iceland, the Faeroe Islands, Ireland and north Britain, Scandinavia, including the upper Baltic, Kola and the whole Siberian coast from Novaya Zemlya to the Bering Strait. After breeding, Tysties only seem to move far enough to avoid being trapped in the ice; a journey of several hundred kilometres, such as from Fair Isle, Shetland, to Essex, is exceptional. Most birds in British waters seem to stay near their breeding stations, which are usually along sea lochs, sounds and other sheltered shores, including some harbours.

The Black Guillemot hauls out on shelving rocks more readily than the Razorbill and Common Guillemot but, although it can stand and walk quite well, it often rests like them on its shanks. The flight, low over the water, has the whirring action common to all the short-winged, stout-bodied auks and requires a pattering take-off. Tysties dive freely, using both legs and wings for propulsion. The food ranges from fish, especially the slippery butterfish *Pholis* species, to small crustaceans, molluscs, marine worms and some seaweed, all obtained in shallow water.

Displays are both individual and communal. Pairs pirouette round each other on the water, and on land, head to tail and uttering a shrill but rather feeble *peee*. This seems to be a general-purpose note, though showing some variation, including E. A. Armstrong's terminal 'wheezy sigh'. The red gape presumably has a function

too when the bill is open. Head-bobbing is a ritualized courtship action (Æ. Petersen) but birds also perform 'displacement' activities such as dipping their bills, bathing and standing up to flap their wings, and these may spread throughout a whole group. Members of a pair chase each other above, along or below the surface of the water and this may also 'infect' other pairs. A communal performance, which may not be display in the accepted sense, is for the whole party, perhaps representing a small breeding

group, to swim gently in one direction in a wavering line, which suddenly turns to move at a new angle. Swimming in line continues after breeding and even into midwinter (Armstrong).

Black Guillemots return to their breeding stations from February onwards in the south. A few up to several thousand pairs may choose sites close together under boulders on the shore, in crevices or in rabbit and other burrows some distance above it, sometimes 2 or 3 km. inland, as in Svalbard. Drainage holes are regularly used in some harbours and odd sites have been in moored boats or even an old cannon; stone

'houses' have been successful in Shetland (R. J. Tulloch). Normally 2 eggs are laid in a scrape lined with small pebbles; they are whitish to pale blue-green or buff, with heavy dark reddish-brown spots, and blotches and grey markings; the nest may be up to 2 m. from the entrance but is occasionally visible. Both sexes share incubation, often from the first egg, though the second is usually laid 3 days later. The chicks, clad in silky blackish down, hatch in about 29 days (Petersen) and show an orange pink gape to their attentive parents; they soon echo the adults' wheezy whistle. They leave the nest at about 37 days old, before they are fully fledged.

Operation Seafarer considered this a difficult species to census because of the hidden nests, but intimate knowledge of the diurnal pattern of attendance at the colony probably allows the Black Guillemot to be censused more accurately than any other North European auk (Ævar Petersen). The 1969-70 breeding population for Britain and Ireland was put at 8340 pairs, probably on the low side. The majority (over 4500 pairs) were in Orkney and Shetland; practically none breed on the east side of Britain and there are only single stations in England and Wales.

Fratercula arctica
PUFFIN
ALCIDAE 30 cm. (20 cm. high)

Tammie Noorie and Coulterneb are 2 north British names which evoke the Puffin's droll appearance. But its almost human look secured it no immunity from seafowl gatherers and Puffins are still harvested in the Faeroe Islands. Its outstanding feature is the roughly triangular, deeply compressed yellow, red and blue bill, to which are added red-rimmed eyes with small blue-grey 'plates' above and below, orange-red legs and webbed feet. The facial adornments are shed after breeding, the smaller bill becomes yellower and so do the legs. The juvenile has duskier cheeks, a narrower grey-brown bill and flesh-coloured legs. The sexes are alike, though males average heavier.

The Puffin has a fast shallow wing-beat and, smaller than Razorbills and guillemots, seems to whirr through the air, spreading its legs to land or splashing head-first on to the sea. Its pale cheeks distinguish it at a distance from other North European auks.

Almost the whole north-western coastline of Europe down to Brittany is in the Puffin's breeding range; it stretches north to Iceland, the arctic archipelagos and to Greenland, with colonies in eastern North America down to Maine; 2 races, *arctica* and *grabae* (mainly British Isles) have been separated. Puffins winter at sea, dispersing from their more northern breeding areas; British-ringed birds have occurred in the western Mediterranean, and a few have crossed the Atlantic. Return to the colonies begins in mid-March in the south; numbers build up offshore, but it may take several weeks before the birds overcome their fear of the land.

Moving easily on land, the Puffin usually stands up on stretched tarsi. As they arrive already paired, the birds' main displays are mutual, with rubbing or clashing of bills, bobbing of heads, gaping and a sort of pattering dance. There is also a 'water dance' when up to 6 birds may swim round each other. The usual call, uttered in various situations, is a growling croak. Puffins feed mainly on small fish, especially sand eels and sprats; hunting may take them 80 km. from their colonies. They propel themselves under water with their wings. Their remarkable trick is to hold up to 11 fish, weighing perhaps 20 g., crosswise between the mandibles.

Puffin colonies are traditionally enormous; the birds burrow into turf-clad banks and slopes of cliffs and small islands; they also occupy cracks in cliff-faces and holes under boulders. Burrows may be 20 cm. to 2 m. long; at the end is a sparsely lined nest scrape where, from late April until June, a (normally) single lightly marked white egg is laid. The parents share incubation, in spells of about 24 hours, for some 6 weeks; then they feed the dusky-downed chick 6 to 9 times a day. After about 40 days feeding ceases; the chick's weight begins to drop and 10 days later it leaves the burrow for the sea.

The Puffin's worst enemy is the Great Black-backed Gull. Many juveniles are caught at the burrow's mouth and colonies on level ground are more at risk than those on slopes. But pollution of some kind, from direct fouling by oil to contamination of food or water, is probably responsible for the huge decreases reported recently. Although a very difficult bird to census, Operation Seafarer estimated the 1969–70 breeding population of Britain and Ireland 'at some 490,000 pairs', against former conjectures of 3 million pairs on St Kilda alone. Research has so far failed to pin down heavy metal or organochlorine pollution as causes of the decline, but rubber threads have been found in Puffins' gizzards, indicating the bizarre hazards that birds face from the throwaway society.

OPPOSITE *Group of Puffins in summer*
BELOW *Winter adults of Little Auk (below) and Puffin (above)*

Plautus alle
LITTLE AUK
ALCIDAE 20 cm.

Smallest of the North Atlantic seabirds and endemic to the region, the Little Auk has been numbered in millions in some of its colonies and may be one of the most numerous birds in the world. In their winter plumages (shown together above) it might be confused with the Puffin, or, because of its size, with young Razorbills and guillemots; but the stubby black bill is characteristic. In summer the head and throat become black-brown with the rest of the upper parts.

Breeding on islands and archipelagos in the
Arctic Ocean, Little Auks or Dovekies spread in
autumn to the south and are sometimes blown
inland in north-western Europe by gales. They
have the typical whirring flight of the family and
chatter incessantly at their colonies. They use
their wings under water when chasing crustaceans and other small marine animals.

Colonies are mainly on sea cliffs or talus
slopes, sometimes several kilometres inland. A
single egg (usually), bluish in ground, is laid
about a metre inside a cavity. Both sexes incubate it for $3\frac{1}{2}$ weeks and feed the chick, which
flies in about 20 days.

Eremophila alpestris
SHORE LARK
ALAUDIDAE 16·5 cm.

In Northern Europe the Shore Lark, a passerine 'song-bird', has a similar regime to some of the waders already described, breeding inland on the alpine tundra and wintering by the sea on low-lying shores. The male in summer has a striking appearance, with his facial pattern of black and yellow surmounted by 2 small but erectile 'horns' – hence the American name, Horned Lark – set off by the generally pinkish-brown wings and upper parts, shading into white under parts. The tail is darker brown with not very conspicuous whitish outer feathers. The female's head pattern is duller and she has no horns, nor does the male in winter. The juvenile looks altogether browner, with yellowish spots on the upper parts. The future head pattern is only faintly indicated; the chin and throat are pale yellow.

The Shore Lark's world breeding distribution is remarkable, covering almost all North America, with a southern enclave in Colombia. In the Old World the range is both desert and montane from North Africa to the Himalayas. But these populations are completely separated from that which breeds from Scandinavia along the north coast of Eurasia to at least 160°E. Linnaeus, as K. H. Voous points out, did not know the Shore Lark in Europe, so its occupation of the Scandinavian fells probably dates from about 1800; in 1973 a pair almost certainly bred in northern Scotland. The main wintering area is along the sandy coasts of the North Sea and Baltic.

Although Shore Larks can hop, they normally walk or run, often associating with Lapland, *Calcarius lapponicus*, and Snow Buntings, *Plectrophenax nivalis*, in winter, when the flock works quietly over the wrack line looking for small crustaceans and molluscs, or visits the coastal marshes and fields in search of seeds and shoots. In summer the principal diet is of insects, especially flies and beetles, and their larvae. Shore Larks rise with shrill calls rather like those of the Meadow Pipit, *Anthus pratensis*, but more musical. The song, delivered at its best from the ground, is a sweet-toned warble; on the wing it forms an element in the undulating, often sustained display flight.

The nest is a small cup of dead stems, lined with plant down and hair and often with a 'forecourt' of pebbles or mammal droppings. Sometimes sheltered by a tussock or stone, it can be very hard to see. The clutch is usually of 4 pale greenish-white eggs, speckled with brown, and laid from the end of May. The female alone incubates, and the chicks hatch in long yellowish down after 10 to 14 days. Fed by both parents, they leave the nest in 9 to 14 days. There are usually 2 broods in a season.

Anthus spinoletta
ROCK/WATER PIPIT
MOTACILLIDAE 16 cm.

This is the passerine most completely adapted to a littoral life, though the 2 races breeding in Northern Europe, the British *petrosus* and Scandinavian *littoralis*, may be derived from the montane Water Pipits. Rock Pipits look darker, more olive-brown or olive-grey and less strongly streaked with black than the Meadow Pipit, *A. pratensis*, with which they often overlap. Also the outer tail feathers are smoky grey, not white and the legs are dark, not pale brown. Juveniles are more streaked than adults. In summer Scandinavian birds tend to show a pinkish flush on the throat and breast, where they are less streaked. Water Pipits in summer have a pronounced pink flush, white superciliary stripe and outer tail feathers, and greyish upper parts. But in Northern Europe they usually occur on migration inland.

The breeding range of the 2 Rock Pipit races runs from Brittany, Ireland and Britain, except the south-east, to Scandinavia north of the Baltic and the Kola Peninsula. This covers all the rocky coastline of Northern Europe, the preferred breeding habitat. On sandy shores the Meadow Pipit replaces the Rock Pipit, but in its absence, on the Isles of Scilly for example, Rock Pipits may take over and nest some way inland. They also frequent lowlying shores in winter, but the British race is sedentary and Scandinavian birds only retreat from the more inhospitable parts of their range and are found on the North Sea coasts and sometimes inland.

Rock Pipits habitually lurk about the wrack lines and upper shore, rising with a *tsup* call, 'rather fuller, more metallic and less squeaky than Meadow Pipit's' (B. W. Tucker). This is to be distinguished from the shrill *chip* of birds with young. The song is also fuller, more musical and more emphatic than the Meadow Pipit's; it is delivered in falling flight after the male has risen almost vertically and may last from 5 seconds to half a minute; it is uttered on the ground as well. Rock Pipits probe the shore for a variety of animal and vegetable food, from insects, adult or larval, to worms, slugs, snails, crustaceans and molluscs, and some seeds. They do not flock so much as aggregate in good feeding areas, often with wagtails and Meadow Pipits.

The nest, built by the female, is usually well hidden in a rocky recess or crevice, sometimes in a wall or breastwork, also on steep banks under vegetation; it is made of dead stems with a fine lining and sometimes white feathers. The 4 to 5 off-white eggs, heavily freckled with brown or grey, are laid from early April in the south and incubated by the female for about 2 weeks. The young are hatched in brownish-grey down, fed by both parents, and fledge in about 16 days. There are normally 2 broods in a season.

Adult Shore Larks in foreground, female (left) and male (right). Behind, winter adults of Scandinavian Rock Pipit (top), Water Pipit (centre) and Rock Pipit (below)